SCHOOLS COUNCIL WORKING PAPER 69

Statistics in schools 11–16: a review

report of the Schools Council
Statistical Education Project

PETER HOLMES
RAMESH KAPADIA
G. NEIL RUBRA
edited by DAPHNE TURNER

Methuen Educational

First published 1981 for the Schools Council
160 Great Portland Street, London W1N 6LL
by Methuen Educational
11 New Fetter Lane, London EC4P 4EE

Filmset by
Northumberland Press Ltd
Gateshead, Tyne and Wear
Printed in Great Britain by
Richard Clay (The Chaucer Press) Ltd
Bungay, Suffolk

British Library Cataloguing in Publication Data

Schools Council Statistical Education Project
Statistics in schools 11–16. – (Schools Council
Working papers; 69 ISSN 0533–1668)
1. Mathematical statistics – Study and teaching
(Secondary) – England
I. Title   II. Holmes, Peter   III. Kapadia, Ramesh
IV. Rubra, G. Neil   V. Schools Council
519.5'07'1242   QA276.18

ISBN 0–423–50840–7

Contents

'Statistics in Your World'

A major outcome of the project's survey was the production of teaching materials. It became clear to the project team that statistical knowledge was important for all pupils, that growing use was being made of statistics in many areas of the school curriculum and that there was a need for material which taught statistics in a practical, relevant and realistic way linking the subject disciplines. With the help of teachers and pupils in fifty-five trial schools, and a similar number of associate schools, twenty-seven units were tested, evaluated and re-tested. These units, each consisting of teachers' notes and a pupil booklet, are published under the general title, 'Statistics in Your World' (Foulsham Educational, 1980–81). There is also a handbook, *Teaching Statistics 11–16* (Foulsham Educational, 1980), which describes the philosophy of the project, gives reasons for teaching statistics, spells out the hierarchies in elementary statistical concepts and techniques, and shows the breadth of applications in society.

Preface

The Schools Council Statistical Education Project was set up at the University of Sheffield in 1975, initially funded for three years, to investigate statistical education in the age-range 11–16. Its aims were:

1 To assess the present situation in statistical education, regarding content, level, motivation and teachers' attitudes, and to relate these to the position of statistics outside schools.

2 To survey the needs of teachers, whether they are teaching statistics as a specialist subject or working in a related field, and the implications for both initial and in-service needs.

3 To devise detailed proposals for implementation of the teaching ideas.

4 To produce teaching materials such as notes for teachers, descriptions of experiments, worksheets and sets of examples.

In the early stage of the project much time and effort was expended in trying to meet the first two of these aims, and a series of ten project papers covering different aspects was produced by the team members. This report is a summarized compilation of those papers, updated where appropriate.

Chapter I is the report of a survey carried out by the project team in a 10 per cent sample of all secondary schools in England and Wales. It reveals what statistics is taught, by whom, to whom and in what subjects. Chapter II considers the statistical content of examinations at GCE O and AO levels and in CSE, investigating the incidence of topics and the types of examination questions asked. Chapter III looks more closely at the statistics pupils meet in their mathematics and science lessons, while Chapter IV similarly investigates the incidence of statistics in humanities and social science courses. In Chapter V the position of probability and statistics in the primary school is considered – providing a useful guide in assessing the statistical background which may be expected of pupils when they start secondary school.

7

The questionnaire used in the survey is reproduced in the appendices, which also include a review of some standard statistics texts, and a comprehensive list of references for in-service courses, equipment, books and articles all relevant to the teaching of statistics.

It is hoped that anyone looking for information about the current position of statistics teaching in schools or seeking references to guide them to further reading, will find this report both interesting and useful.

I. Survey of statistics teaching in schools

This chapter summarizes the findings of the project's survey of schools by postal questionnaire. Initially a draft questionnaire was sent to fifteen schools and several suggested modifications from this pilot scheme were incorporated in the final version (reproduced in Appendix A). The revised questionnaire was sent to 530 schools involving thirty-eight local education authorities in England and Wales, and including a number of independent schools.

To assess the proportion of schools teaching statistics replies were also needed from schools that were not, and a covering letter stressed the need to provide this information. Also emphasized was the project's interest in statistics taught in all parts of the school curriculum. The response rate was high – 397 replies (75 per cent). Distortions due to non-response were therefore not a major problem.

Examination courses: statistics

Questions were included (in section B) to discover the proportion of schools offering statistics as a specialist examination subject at 16, and the number of pupils entered. Only a small minority of schools entered candidates for public examinations in statistics:

for O level GCE, 31 out of 315 schools (nearly 10 per cent);
for CSE, 22 out of 308 schools (just over 7 per cent)

From these schools the proportion of 16-year-old pupils entered was also a minority, an average of about one in eight for GCE. The mean population entering CSE was about 22 per cent, one pupil in every four or five, but this is a misleading figure as ten of the twenty-two schools entered 10 or 15 per cent of pupils, similar to the GCE proportion, but another eight entered about a third of their pupils, presumably representing whole classes or sets. The distributions are shown in Figure 1. The proportions of all pupils sitting these examinations can be estimated as approximately:

9

O level GCE $10\% \times 12\frac{1}{2}\% = 1\frac{1}{4}\%$
CSE $7\% \times 22\% = 1\frac{1}{2}\%$

Assuming no one pupil takes both, this yields a maximum of $2\frac{3}{4}$ per cent of the school population. Fewer than fifty-three schools altogether prepared for these examinations, as some offered both. Another obstacle to O level is that only three examining boards provide an O-level statistics syllabus, although other boards have A O level syllabuses.

Even the schools with examination courses in statistics see them as a minority interest, and only a small proportion of school children have any opportunity to attempt them.

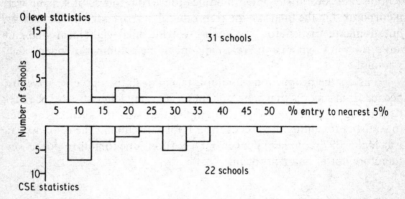

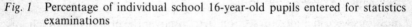

Fig. 1 Percentage of individual school 16-year-old pupils entered for statistics examinations

Examination courses: mathematics and other subjects

Question B2 asked if there were any statistical content in other examination syllabuses. The attempt to provide a compact format to the questionnaire led respondents to run GCE and CSE courses together here; had the mathematics cell been subdivided it would have been possible to establish how many schools are teaching a traditional GCE mathematics syllabus excluding statistics, and how many a more modern syllabus including statistics. All CSE courses fall into the latter group, though the topics taught do not always correspond exactly with those in the published syllabuses. The analysis which follows suggests that 'modern' GCE and CSE candidates may be taught a common syllabus, and sometimes not

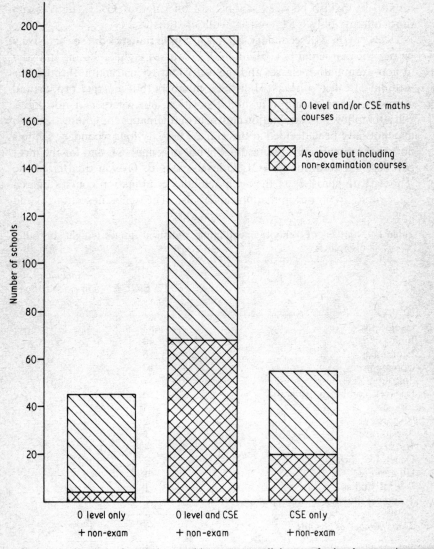

Fig. 2 Distribution of statistics teaching among syllabuses of schools returning questionnaires

segregated, in earlier years. But whereas schools teaching no statistics can be presumed to be using a traditional mathematics GCE course and not offering CSE, where statistics is taught for CSE but not GCE the analysis cannot distinguish between schools not offering any GCE subjects and those offering only CSE courses without statistics.

Twelve of the 318 secondary schools teaching statistics did so exclusively *outside* the mathematics CSE and GCE courses, eight confining statistics to non-examination classes and the other four to instruction through the medium of other subjects. Half these numbers (but a larger proportion) of middle schools were in a similar position, but whether or not pupils will later follow an examination course in mathematics containing statistics may not have been decided at this stage. The sixty-four secondary schools not teaching statistics are presumably not offering CSE and for the most part using a traditional GCE O-level syllabus. Over a quarter of the schools with statistics in their mathematics examination courses offered some topics to non-examination classes also. The replies in sections B and

Table 1 Number of schools mentioning statistical topics taught in other disciplines

	For CSE/GCE courses	Including non-examination courses
Geography	83	110
Biology	48	60
Economics	16 ⎫	22*
Commerce	16 ⎬	
Sociology	7	10
Sciences (combined, general)	10 ⎫	
Physics	3 ⎪	39
Chemistry	2 ⎬	
Agriculture	1 ⎭	
History	4 ⎫	
General studies	2 ⎪	32
Humanities	1 ⎬	
Liberal studies	1 ⎭	
Technical drawing and computing		2
Total number of schools	159	162

* In theory the right-hand column includes the figures from the left-hand column. This would imply that several schools prepare the statistical content of economics and commerce jointly.

D (on course content) do not correspond perfectly, but an attempt to reconcile them gives the pattern of available courses shown in Table 1 and Figure 2. These relate to numbers of schools and have not been weighted according to school size. However, separate analysis of the various strata in the sample does not show any consistent bias between smaller and larger schools or between different types of school.

About a third of the schools teaching some statistics mentioned the presence of statistical ideas in the examination syllabus of one or more other subjects, but half included statistical topics in teaching these subjects. The range of disciplines corresponds well with that found in O-level syllabuses (see page 30). The number of schools quoted (Table 1) is probably an incomplete record of those using statistical concepts and techniques in various disciplines if evidence from GCE and CSE syllabuses and examination boards is taken into account. No doubt the discrepancy results more from difficulties in finding time to locate the right people and persuading them to complete the appropriate sections of the questionnaire than from failure to cover the syllabuses adequately in class.

Course content

Of 397 schools replying, five out of every six taught some statistics (question A4). Of 382 schools with children up to 16 years or more, four out of every five prepared some children for mathematics examinations containing some statistics (question B2). Roughly half the schools offered mathematics courses including statistics for both GCE and CSE, another sixth for CSE but not GCE (either because GCE was not taken or because an older GCE mathematics syllabus without statistics was used), and a further eighth for GCE but not CSE. A few schools ($1\frac{1}{2}$ per cent) showed statistics as being taught only through the medium of other subjects, and of these one in three were middle schools. Over a quarter of the schools teaching statistics also offered it to non-examination mathematics classes. Over a third included some statistical topics in their geography courses also, and about a fifth in their biology courses. Virtually half included statistical work in some part of the curriculum outside the mathematics department. These figures need interpreting with some caution as they may include work primarily designed to facilitate sixth-form studies, and there may be incomplete reporting: it would be rash to suppose that these effects compensate. (See Figure 2 and Table 2.)

Figure 3 shows the distribution of topics taught by frequency of reporting

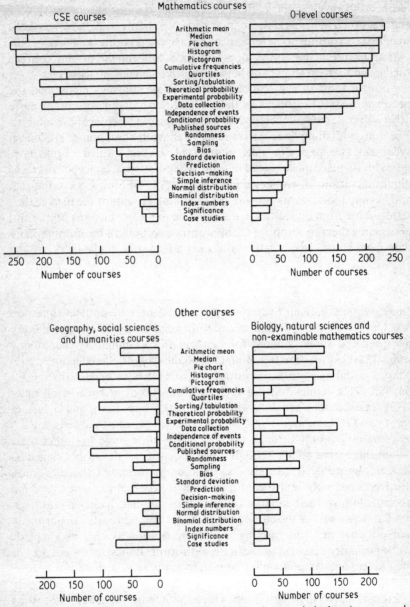

Fig. 3 Number of pre-O-level courses in which various statistical topics are taught

(question D). Although this sounds simple, it does not give comparable results for the statistics teaching within the various disciplines (even assuming no omissions in the replies). The three mathematics syllabuses, GCE, CSE, and non-examination, may in practice all be taught together in one class, at least in the earlier years. The length of the bars represents the number of syllabuses in which the topic occurs, not the number of times it is offered to pupils. Thus the apparent predominance of mathematics in Figure 3 partly reflects the consideration of more than one syllabus in mathematics, an opportunity not given for other subjects. When only one of the mathematics syllabuses is taken, especially in the most popular areas where GCE and CSE are fairly well balanced, the teaching of these topics in other parts of the curriculum is clearly quite significant.

There is a fair area of agreement on the most important topics among all statistics courses, and on some elements in other courses. The applied subjects have raised the ranking by one or two steps in data collection and tabulation, use of published figures, predicting and decision-making and case studies, whereas the more theoretical aspects of probability tend to be found mainly in the mathematics domain. Analysis of dispersion is also left largely to the mathematicians. Although quartiles are treated in more than twice as many mathematics courses as standard deviation, even in these courses the median has not quite attained parity with the mean. Within the twenty-six topics, three-quarters of the courses cover the seven commonest topics, over half cover the most popular twelve, and a quarter at least twenty topics. This means that the point at which courses drop out any further statistics is fairly evenly spread down the list of topics covered, though there are some discontinuities in the steady decline of numbers.

The group of pictorial methods takes pride of place, followed by elementary descriptive measures and data collection. There is a clear separation between elementary probability, encountered in the majority of mathematics courses, and the more sophisticated theoretical topics such as independence, bias, inference, significance, covered in from one-third to one-tenth of courses. At the same time some topics (for example, sampling) occur in more courses than others (for example, bias, randomness) which might desirably be treated together, and the sequence of topics is not in exact descending order of difficulty.

Other topics mentioned by some teachers were: questionnaire design, Lorenz curves, permutations and combinations, standard error of the mean, Poisson distribution, flow charts and climatic statistics.

The subject groupings in Figure 3 also deserve a word of explanation. There was evidence of variation in the thoroughness with which staff of other subjects were canvassed and responded, and some topics and disciplines may be under-represented. Geography and biology each account for over half the entries in their respective groups. These groups were formed partly for ease of exposition but also because some subject groups with distinct designations could be expected to overlap, and coarser grouping was the surest way to avoid boundary problems. Some topics

Table 2 Analysis of mathematics examination courses which include statistics

Schools teaching statistics	Available also in non-examination courses	Not offered in non-examination courses	Total	% of all schools replying
For GCE O level but not CSE	(%) 3 (6½)	43	46	12
For CSE but not GCE O level	20 (30)	45	65	16
For both GCE O level and CSE:				
secondary school	59 ⎱ (30)	136	195 ⎱ 51	
middle schools	7 ⎰	–	7 ⎰	
For non-examination mathematics classes only:				
secondary schools	8	–	8 ⎱ 3	
middle schools	4	–	4 ⎰	
Through the medium of other subjects only:				
secondary schools	4	–	4 ⎱ 1½	
middle schools	2	–	2 ⎰	
Sub-totals	107	224	331	
Schools not teaching statistics				
Secondary schools	–	64	64 ⎱ 17	
Middle schools	–	2	2 ⎰	
Grand total in sample			397	

contain more than one entry from the same school if, for instance, they were taught within two distinct subjects both under the 'social sciences' umbrella. Several subjects were included in the following two groups:

Natural sciences: physics, chemistry, combined science, general science, geology, agricultural studies, technical drawing

Social sciences and humanities: economics, sociology, commerce, computer studies, social studies, integrated/liberal studies, humanities, history, English, government, religious education.

The distribution compiled from question E1 on the number of teachers involved in statistics teaching is recorded in Table 3.

Table 3 Number of teachers involved in statistics teaching

Number of teachers per school	1	2	3	4	5	6	7	8	9	10	11	12	over 12	Total
Number of schools	28	36	47	47	43	45	22	28	7	14	4	6	2	329
% of schools	8·5	10·9	14·3	14·3	13·1	13·7	6·7	8·5	2·1	4·3	1·2	1·8	0·6	
Number of teachers	28	72	141	188	215	270	154	224	63	140	44	72	29	1640
% of teachers	1·7	4·4	8·6	11·5	13·1	16·5	9·4	13·7	3·8	8·5	2·7	4·4	1·8	

The mean number of teachers who take part in statistical work is about five. As the stratification did not specifically take size of school into account, this figure could be affected by the inclusion of a disproportionate number of large or small schools. The median number of teachers teaching statistics per school is five. It can be seen that a small majority of the schools (55 per cent) employ between three and six teachers on statistics tuition.

Figure 4 shows the number of mathematics teachers who also teach statistics. Unfortunately we have no record of how many mathematics teachers these schools employed who did *not* take part in statistics teaching. However, the nature of the distribution and of the asides recorded suggest that the general pattern is to involve most or all of the mathematics teachers in the statistical elements of the course up to fourth-form level rather than to ask one or two teachers to specialize. (The opposite might be expected to apply to sixth-form classes.)

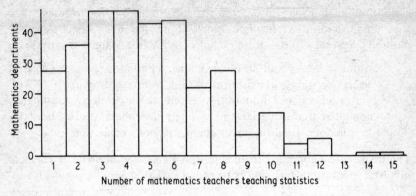

Fig. 4   Number of teachers of statistics in school mathematics departments

How teachers acquired their knowledge of statistics

Again here, the desire to keep the inquiry concise excluded the collection of control data. Moreover, the question on how teachers acquired their knowledge of statistics (E2) proved ambiguous. About three-quarters of the teachers listed (as was intended) only the main source of their knowledge. The remainder included more than one method for at least some of the teachers, so that the total of 1750 qualifications recorded slightly exceeds the 1640 teachers represented (the difference is about 7 per cent). This cannot be presumed an adequate representation of people's additional qualifications and studies; in the replies where the number of qualifications equalled the number of teachers exactly it cannot be assumed that additional relevant studies were invariably absent. It is quite possible that a third or more of all statistics teachers acquired their own knowledge from more than one source. The results obtained for mathematics teachers are given in Table 4 and Figure 5.

As only a small proportion of replies were able to include much detail on the qualifications of teachers outside the mathematics departments, it would be unwise to try to draw any firm conclusions about talent elsewhere in the schools.

The general conclusions that emerge are that degree courses, certificate courses, and self-education provide almost equal shares of the expertise among present statistics-teaching staff (roughly one-third attributable to the first and 30 per cent to each of the others). In-service courses have played a relatively small part, more as an additional than a primary

Staff shortage

Out of 314 schools answering question E3 on staff shortage, 277 did not consider themselves handicapped by lack of talent to teach statistics in existing mathematics courses (about 88 per cent). However, quite a number felt that staff resources were not sufficient to teach all the statistical topics they considered desirable. This could mean, for instance, that some schools were inhibited from designing a Mode III CSE course in statistics. Many felt that scope exists for non-examination courses in practical and applied statistics using projects or case studies, which would benefit from the appointment of staff with appropriate experience.

Books and accessories to statistics teaching

The *textbooks* mentioned most frequently in answers to question C1 are shown in Figure 6. (Forty-six other textbooks were mentioned.)

Many schools mentioned more than one title, though how often these were used together or in parallel classes (for lack of copies) was not ascertained. Of the two SMP series, thirty-six schools listed both A to H and 1 to 5 in this way. Of the 330 schools replying to this section, 181 (55 per cent) were using SMP books, and of all replies (including non-statistics schools) over 45 per cent. At the other end of the scale, two schools mentioned the *Annual Abstract of Statistics*, one *Whitaker's Almanac*, and at least one quoted *Which?* It is possible that this under-represents the use of reference books if the phrase 'textbooks' was interpreted strictly by some respondents. Very few textbooks were listed as used within other subjects, and none of these was mentioned by more than one school. The preponderance of mathematics books in the list, and the poor showing of specialist statistics books, seems to confirm that most schools treat statistics as part of a mathematics course rather than a specialist subject in its own right.

Very few sets of published *work cards* were mentioned. The SMP cards were used by thirty-one (9 per cent) of the schools. Other series mentioned were *Maths Pack* (Cassells), Nuffield Mathematics Project *Problem Cards* (Chambers & Murray) and the Scottish *Modular Mathematics* sets (Heinemann). Twenty other schools said they used published work cards but did not specify which.

Not many schools were using material from other Schools Council projects – Mathematics for the Majority and/or its continuation project were mentioned by twelve schools; Geography for the Young School Leaver (six schools); Geography 14–16 (four schools); and Schools Council Integrated Science Project (SCISP) (three schools). Nuffield Secondary Science, Nuffield Biology and Oxford Geography were also mentioned (two schools each).

Published *case studies* are clearly difficult to find. Items mentioned included newspaper articles (twelve schools), census data (two schools) and insurance tables (one school). None of these is strictly a case study, though it was of value to have them included in the replies. Eight schools acknowledged using published case studies without being more specific.

A great deal of ingenuity goes into devising and using ancillary materials to teach statistics. Figure 7 is a guide to the nature of the material in use. The numbers show how many schools mentioned each particular item, but relying, as many of them must, on what springs to the respondent's mind, they doubtless under-represent the true quantities, and may not accurately reflect the true proportions between one device and another.

Thirty schools said that they used *posters*. Those specified were posters produced by Pictorial Cards Educational Trust, National Savings, local authority rates departments, banks, Shell Education and Educational Supply Association (ESA). Only eight schools said they used *films*. No titles were mentioned. The most frequently used television series for teaching

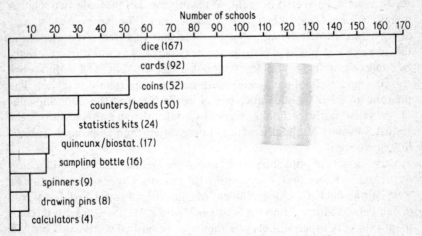

Other items mentioned were: roulette wheels, weights, nailboards, darts, thermometers, poppet beads, telephone directory, straws, stopwatch, scales and punched cards

Fig. 7   Ancillary material used in teaching statistics

statistics was *Countdown** (twenty-eight schools – $8\frac{1}{2}$ per cent). *Mathshow** was mentioned by one school. Twenty-one other schools said they used television programmes but did not specify which series; some may select particular programmes rather than follow a complete course.

'HOME-MADE' MATERIAL

Home-made equipment mentioned in question C2 included dice, biased dice, cards, counters, spinners, posters, nail mazes, polyhedra, sample boxes, seed box, darts and target, flowcharts for geography, sampling rods, cotton-reel holder for displays, coloured beads in jars, balls, a sampling disc and electrical circuits.

Some of the material mentioned reflected the concern to relate statistics teaching to everyday life. Schools listed items such as questionnaires, simulations and games (particularly in geography), using data from field trips, a local farm and the P E department, traffic surveys, use of data on items such as climate, trade and food and even the counting of worms. This concern to make statistics relevant, and the fact that much of the material for this comes under the 'home-made' label, may indicate the lack of really good published material of this type. The questions and descriptions were not detailed enough to show whether people made their own equipment to incorporate superior features, or for the educational value of the making itself, or simply from lack of funds or time to buy the versions on the market.

Additional resources

Twelve items were suggested in question E4 as of possible use in statistics teaching and 308 schools ticked at least one of them on the mathematics side. The number of schools ticking each item varied from 246 for national in-service courses to 291 for a reference source book. In general, the items ticked most often were also the most popular on the three-point scale. It seems that teachers occasionally ignored those items they felt would be of little or no use. Thus it is likely that the last few items should have lower scores.

The average score for each item was computed as a weighted mean:

$$(n_1 \cdot 0 + n_2 \cdot 1 + n_3 \cdot 2)/(n_1 + n_2 + n_3)$$

---

* *Countdown* and *Mathshow* are no longer being televised. Details about the availability of current schools television programmes concerned with statistics are given in Appendix C.

where n_1 ticked 0, n_2 ticked 1 and n_3 ticked 2. Thus the maximum possible is 2, the minimum is zero. The results are shown in Table 5.

Only 130 schools ticked in the column for other departments. No doubt in some schools the form did not reach other departments. Besides it is rather difficult for other departments as a whole to have a view on, say, the usefulness of work cards in statistics teaching – this would naturally vary from one subject to another. This must be borne in mind when assessing the results for these questions.

Table 5   Analysis of useful resources

NUMBER TICKING	MATHEMATICS DEPARTMENTS		RESOURCE	OTHER DEPARTMENTS	
	Average	*Sum*		*Average*	*Sum*
291	1·37	399	Reference source book	1·40	117
284	1·33	378	Work cards	0·96	102
270	1·10	298	Theoretical material	0·99	96
284	1·05	299	Pamphlets on topics	0·96	106
270	0·99	268	Films	0·93	96
283	0·93	264	New textbooks	0·83	98
270	0·91	246	Pamphlets on subjects	1·17	116
273	0·87	238	Local in-service courses	1·10	102
261	0·86	225	Case studies	1·08	110
253	0·82	208	Videotapes	0·8	95
250	0·74	185	Tape/slides	0·78	87
246	0·56	138	National in-service courses	0·61	89

The most requested items were a reference source book and work cards for experiments. Theoretical material and pamphlets on topics were also popular. Other departments were understandably keen on pamphlets on subjects (for example, statistics in history). Local in-service courses were preferred to national ones. Surprisingly teachers were not particularly keen on visual aids such as tape/slides or films; perhaps they felt the cost was prohibitive or the effort in setting up and organizing the use of such aids was not worthwhile.

There were only a few replies to question E5 on what other help would be welcome. Teachers wanted more time and money; they also asked for up-to-date source material. A few requested an examination in statistics (there are a few, as listed in Chapter II). A few schools wanted specialist teachers for statistics.

Needs of pupils

Surprisingly 81 per cent of schools felt that the statistical needs of the majority of pupils are adequately met by the age of 16 (question E6). From our analysis of syllabuses and courses, described later, and from other information gleaned from the questionnaire, we are not convinced of this. Respondents may have taken a narrower view than intended of the role and scope of statistical thought, perhaps because it is a rather new subject. This came out in some of the omissions listed by those who felt that school statistical education was inadequate. Teachers felt that project work would be useful, particularly in illustrating practical applications such as advertising and interpretation of surveys. A host of other ideas were listed; some of these are described more fully later.

Statistics for pupils at 16-plus

Question F2 asked all schools, including those who professed to teach no statistics, whether it would be worth investigating problems in the teaching of statistics to pupils at 16-plus. Ten per cent did not reply, including a fair number who felt unable to comment as they had no sixth form, though many schools without sixth forms did reply. Altogether 75 per cent felt that it would be worthwhile; 15 per cent did not. If we exclude those schools who did not reply, 83 per cent felt that such work would be valuable while 17 per cent did not. One teacher commented that it was 'Worthwhile but *not* worth a great deal of research funds', which depends on what is meant by a great deal!

As a whole the answers suggest much support for further work at sixth-form level. Many of those schools who teach no statistics at all for the 11–16 age-range were in favour, as they felt that there were important outstanding problems in sixth-form statistics.

Teachers' general comments

We have purposely left question F1 to the last: it was the rather open question inviting general comments on hopes, fears, complaints, problems, etc. It is not possible to give a fair summary of 160 comments without reproducing each one. A few with individual appeal are picked out, with no attempt to present an overall viewpoint.

Some general comments on statistics teaching:

It is a topic which has relevance in everyday life. The children find it interesting and therefore it is a relatively easy subject to teach [at CSE level].

It is, even at a non-academic level, useful in protecting girls against unfounded claims in advertising, etc., and arouses discrimination. Girls appreciate information provided by graphical methods where they would shy away from tabulated figures.

Apart from the usual obvious benefits, it develops skill in basic number work, accuracy in checking and an understanding of various graphs.

Many adults are completely unaware of uses (or abuses!) of statistics, which in itself is bad, and propagates the idea of their being used to deceive others. The better the subject is taught the more freely our next generation will be able to choose which 'facts' to believe.

Statistics should be presented in context and not as an end in itself.

The pocket calculator revolutionizes the whole thing, making the processing of real data really straightforward. Statistical library programs on computers should be used more widely.

Suggestions on experiments which are both real, short-time and subjectable to elementary analysis would be valuable.

Nevertheless not all comments are positive:

In general it is being taught efficiently, research seems wasteful.

On the age/ability range there is a conflict of opinion:

At my present school statistics is being taught to a high ability group who are capable of O level. Other schools I have taught in have tended to regard statistics as something for the 'left-overs', i.e. those who are not going to take either O level or CSE.

Not only is a wide range of conceptual complexity available but any project will enable pupils within a group to find their own role and level, and concrete, purposeful practice in basic manipulations is provided for all.

One comment betrayed resentment:

The biggest error in statistics is supposing that putting together the results of questionnaires, where inevitably every answer should be qualified in some way, will produce some picture of the real situation. Any attempt to answer social or educational questions by this method is doomed to failure.

A plea struck a sympathetic chord:

This year we offered our present 3rd year a preliminary choice for the subsequent year in statistics. Very few indicated interest, we need to do a PR job!

Though there is hope:

A change of attitude is taking place. Ten years ago we taught no statistics at all. We may soon use O-level statistics for some boys.

For other subjects:

More liaison between departments would facilitate a better understanding of collected data.

Still falling between maths and current affairs when the former haven't sufficient time and the latter insufficient scope.

However:

The statistical approach in non-mathematical subjects is influenced by the personal adequacy of the teachers concerned.

Is this comment from another school an answer?:

(a) Increased contact between local schools ... best chaired initially by a member of the Schools Council Project, (b) contact with university or polytechnic, etc., to see the kinds of requirements needed for statistics degrees, etc., (c) regular meetings between the three groups mentioned previously (i) industry, (ii) university, polytechnic, etc., (iii) schools.

II. Statistics in examinations

GCE O-level syllabuses

Statistical ideas occur in many syllabuses of many subjects. They are considered here under three headings: statistics, mathematics, and other subjects. The statistical syllabus content for O and AO statistics and mathematics syllabuses is analysed in Table 6 which needs to be read with a certain amount of care. As far as possible terms which occur in the printed syllabus are reproduced in the list, but there are exceptions. Syllabuses which refer to the use of working mean and class interval in calculating means are grouped with those which refer to the mean of $aX + b$; weighted means are put together with index numbers. Clearly not all syllabuses are as detailed as each other. A reference to, for instance, representation of data may refer to some or all of the following: bar chart, pie chart, frequency polygon, histogram. The full extent of the implications of a syllabus can only be deduced from a long-term look at the question papers set. The table divides the syllabuses into four sections: the three O-level statistics syllabuses; the statistical parts of O-level mathematics syllabuses; AO-level syllabuses in statistics, and mathematics or mathematics with statistics.

STATISTICS

The three O-level statistics syllabuses are produced by the Associated Examining Board (A1), the Southern Universities Joint Board (S1) and the Welsh Joint Education Committee (W1). Of these the Welsh syllabus is stated as being for 'mature' students, and is intended as a one-year course for 16-year-old pupils. It is noticeable that when compared with the mathematics syllabuses below, these syllabuses do refer more to the problems of collecting and classifying data, to the use of statistics in social contexts such as index numbers and birth and death rates, and to generally

28

used statistical ideas such as regression and correlation, as well as to the usual statistical techniques involved in calculations. Although there is no specific reference to inference, phrases on question papers such as 'Explain why the graph has this form', 'When, approximately, do you think the employees' wages were increased?' do show that pupils are intended to think critically about the data and make simple inferences. It is disappointing that such phrases do not occur more often.

In the A O section the two University Entrance and School Examinations Council (University of London) papers 875 and 872 (L3 and L4), make up a very substantial statistics syllabus, as does the A EB Additional Statistics (A2) particularly since this includes the A1 syllabus. The Oxford and Cambridge School Examinations Board syllabus in statistics (OC1) is the statistical section of their A-level Mathematics with Statistics syllabus, and clearly requires a great deal of maturity on the part of its students. The Cambridge University Local Examinations Syndicate A O syllabus in statistics (C3) is interesting in that it is the only one to have a compulsory project as part of its requirements. A list of suggested project titles is available from the Syndicate offices in Cambridge.

MATHEMATICS

Many of the older mathematical syllabuses include some such phrase as 'graphical representation of data'. These have not been included in this list which is basically the more recent O-level mathematics syllabuses containing work on probability and statistics. It is clear, both from the syllabuses and the papers set, that there is much more emphasis here on arithmetical and mathematical techniques, and much less on the origins and uses of statistics. There is usually little attempt to keep the statistics in the questions in context, or to ask the more general type of question which requires interpretation of data. Perhaps this is only to be expected since the papers are for a mathematics O level and need to measure the mathematical abilities of the candidates. The only exception to these comments is the Joint Matriculation Board's Commercial Mathematics paper (J3). ME1 (St Dunstan's) includes topics listed in the optional supplementary syllabus.

At the AO level the general tendency is to include also some of the early mathematical statistics ideas from the A-level syllabuses – the use of $aX + b$, some specific distributions such as the binomial, and permutations and combinations. The Oxford and Cambridge Board's syllabus,

Mathematics for Biology (OC3), reflects its specialist nature by including regression, confidence limits, and the use of the t distribution and χ^2 test.

OTHER SUBJECTS

Statistical ideas come (explicitly or implicitly) into almost any subject where quantification is being considered. The main aspects of the curriculum which at present do not contain statistical ideas are English, languages (but see below), art and craft, music. One can, of course, point to ideas such as the use of random ideas in some modern music, or the use of statistical tests as part of the consideration of authorship of texts, but such ideas do not seem to arise naturally within the context of published syllabuses. It would clearly be impracticable to give a complete breakdown of syllabuses as for the previous two sections. Instead the items that arise are considered under three headings: those that specifically use statistics, those that could possibly use statistics, and those that will use statistics when pursued in more depth (in a more advanced or more academic course). The lines between these categories are not easily drawn. No attempt has been made to cover all the references, just sufficient to indicate the scope and source of topics.*

Items which specifically use statistics
A fairly common rubric in many syllabuses refers to questions being set involving the interpretation of statistical material. This applies to Geography (many), General Science (W), Use of English (A), General Studies (A), Government, Economics and Commerce (J), Integrated Science (L), Human Biology (J), and others. Biology (C) expects candidates to interpret unfamiliar data and draw conclusions from their interpretation. This syllabus also expects candidates to know about methods of survey, including quadrats and capture-recapture, estimation of frequency, density, percentage cover, quantitative sampling and collecting methods. Religious Studies (L) draws candidates' attention to 'the following material which may be relevant . . . (v) statistical data'. This is in the context of social

---

* Abbreviations used here for the GCE examination boards are the same as in Table 6: Associated Examining Board (A), Cambridge University Local Examinations Syndicate (C), Joint Matriculation Board (J), University Entrance and School Examinations Council, University of London (L), Oxford Delegacy of Local Examinations (O), Oxford and Cambridge Schools Examination Board (OC), Southern Universities Joint Board (S), Welsh Joint Education Committee (W).

and moral problems such as marriage, divorce, work, leisure, money, hunger, poverty, population growth and war.

Various references to population clearly involve the use of collected statistics, so we have world hunger and world population (Biology (A and OC), Geography (J) and others), population and its distribution (Geography (many), Economics (many)), population trends (Social Economics (A), Sociology (A)), birth rate (Integrated Science (L)), population changes in Great Britain (History) (S)). Most biologically oriented syllabuses include references to genetics, heredity and Mendelian inheritance. Some take this into practical fields such as breeding and stock improvement, the application of scientific principles to farming – for example, Rothamsted (History of Agriculture (A)), gene frequency in populations and random fertilization (Biology (S)). Some biological subjects bring out the connexion between health and the environment – for example, housing conditions and overcrowding (Human Biology (W)), the data which relate lung diseases to air pollution and smoking (General Science (W)), the measurement of growth rates and influencing factors (Biology (S)).

Much statistical work can come from the economics of everyday life (General Studies (A)), with index of retail prices (Economic Principles (A), Integrated Humanities (J)), government planning, sources of information and opinion polls (Social Economics (A)), taxation and pensions (Economic History (A)), inflation (History (O), (C)), insurance (Commerce (many)), growth of national product (Economic and Public Affairs (S)), cost and choice of foods (Food and Nutrition (S)) and renting or buying a house (Home Economics (S)), while Social Science (J) provides a comprehensive test of statistical techniques in the practise situation.

Statistical methods in business come in through business risks (Social Economics (A)), estimates (Building Practice (A)), market research (Commerce (S), (C)), average stock and stock turnover (Bookkeeping (J)).

Other items in this section include distribution of temperature and rainfall (Geography (many)), simulation of queues (Computer Studies (O)), poverty surveys (Sociology (O)), statistical recording of imports and exports (Commerce (C)), distribution of parliamentary seats (History (A)) and the exhaustion of natural resources (Geography (L)).

Items which could use statistics
Several syllabuses include the possibility of projects, and many of these could involve a statistical element.

Many social problems come under this heading. It is possible to discuss them all qualitatively, but the use of collected statistics keeps the discussion more in touch with reality. These include problems of old age, housing, crime and punishment (Religious Studies (A) and others), poverty (Social Economics (A), History (C)), social conditions (Economic History (A), Human Biology (J)), equal pay (History (L)), standards of living (History (S), (O)), employment levels (History (S), (C)), racial problems (World Affairs (S), Sociology (O)), consumer protection (Commerce (S)), social mobility (Sociology (O), History (L)), drug addiction and alcoholism (Human Biology (A), (L)), social services (many).

Biological topics include pest control, the relation of breathing and pulse rate to exercise (Biology (W)), smoking and its effect on health (Human Biology (W), (A)), the town water supply (Human Biology (W), (O), (L), Geography (A)), health hazards of sound and vibration (General Science (W)), medical discoveries (Economic History (A)), simple fertilizer trials (Biology (A), (S)), crops in relation to climate and soils (Biology (A), Environmental Science (C)), dispersal of seeds (Botany (O)) and crop distribution (Geography (J)), disease control with reference to the world problem (Biology (OC), Environmental Science (C)), transmission of disease (Human Biology (O), (S), (J)), effectiveness of vaccination, immunity (Human Biology (many)), birth control (Environmental Studies (A), Integrated Science (L), Human Biology (L)), personal, family and community health (Human Biology (J)), conservation with reference, for example, to overfishing (Biology (L)) and Environmental Pollution (many).

Several problems of government and business come under this heading. There is British overseas trade (many), balance of trade and payment (many), insurance and risks of business (Commerce (W), Social Economics (A), History (S)), advertising (Social Economics (A), Commerce (S), (O), (C)), transport (many Geography and History), industrial growth (Economic History (A)), economic and social effects of wars and the depression (History (O), (C)), growth of towns (Geography (many)), the tourist industry (Geography (OC)), migration, immigration and emigration (History (many)), voting patterns (Sociology (O)), income, supply of labour, sales promotion, stock purchasing and warehousing (Government Economics and Commerce (J)).

Other items in this section include tourism and social life in France (Modern Languages (A), French Life and Literature (S)), prosperity and affluence in Germany (Modern Languages (A)), sources of new material and energy (Physical Chemistry (L)), factors affecting horticultural enterprise (Agricultural Science (O)), bias in historical evidence (History (L)),

Key to syllabuses in Table 6

L1	Syllabus B (361)	
L2	Syllabus C (362)	University Entrance and
L3	Statistical Additional O level (875)	School Examinations Council,
L4	Pure Mathematics with Probability Additional O level (872)	University of London

W1	Statistics O level	Welsh Joint Education Committee
W2	Additional Mathematics O level	

A1	Statistics O level (063)	
A2	Additional Statistics O level (185) (also includes syllabus for A1)	
A3	Mathematics Commercial, paper 3, O level (102/3)	Associated Examining Board
A4	Additional Mathematics, paper 2, Statistics O level (188/2)	

J1	Mathematics syllabus C O level	
J2	Additional Mathematics (Pure Mathematics with Statistics) Alternative O level (AO)	Joint Matriculation Board
J3	Commercial Mathematics O level	

OC1	Statistics AO level	
OC2	General Mathematics AO level	Oxford and Cambridge School
OC3	Mathematics for Biology AO level	Examinations Board

S1	Statistics O level	
S2	Mathematics syllabus B O level	
S3	Mathematics and Statistics for Commerce O level	Southern Universities Joint Board
S4	Additional Mathematics (statistics option) AO level	

O1	Mathematics (part ii statistics option) O level (051)	Oxford Delegacy of Local
O2	Mathematics O level (052)	Examinations
O3	Additional Mathematics O level (053)	

C1	Mathematics syllabus C O level (453)	
C2	Additional Mathematics O level (471)	Cambridge University Local
C3	Statistics (includes a project) AO level (962)	Examinations Syndicate

ME1	MEI (St Dunstan's) syllabus O level
ME2	MEI Additional Mathematics
SM1	Schools Mathematics Project syllabuses N and C (statistics content identical) O level
SM2	SMP Additional Mathematics (includes syllabus for SM1) O level
MM	Midlands Mathematics Experiment O level

Table 6 Analysis of syllabuses

TOPIC	O LEVEL																	ADDITIONAL OR ALTERNATIVE O LEVEL														
	Statistics			*Mathematics*														*Statistics*				*Mathematics*										
	A1	S1	W1	L1	L2	A3	J1	J3	ME1	S2	S3	O1	O2	C1	SM1	MM	A2	OC1	C3	L3	A4	J2	L4	OC2	OC3	O3	C2	ME2	S4	SM2	W2
Critical appreciation															1																
Statistical inquiries																															
Collection of data	1	1	1				1							1		1	1	1	1		1		1		1	1	1	1			
Census methods	1	1	1														1	1	1		1		1								
Classification of data							1	1	1	1							1	1	1		1								1		
Sampling methods	1	1	1				1							1			1	1	1		1		1		1	1	1	1			
Tabulation	1	1	1				1			1						1	1	1	1		1		1					1			
Questionnaires	1	1	1														1	1	1		1										
Misuse of statistics	1	1	1					1									1	1	1		1		1								
Bias in sampling	1	1					1										1	1	1		1								1		
Discrete distributions	1	1	1	1	1	1	1	1	1	1	1	1	1	1	1	1	1	1	1	1	1	1	1	1	1	1	1	1	1		1
Continuous distributions	1	1	1	1	1	1	1	1	1	1	1	1	1	1	1	1	1	1	1	1	1	1	1	1	1	1	1				
Representation of data	1	1	1	1	1	1	1	1	1	1	1	1	1	1	1	1	1	1	1	1	1	1	1	1	1	1	1	1	1		1
Bar charts	1	1	1	1	1	1	1	1	1	1	1	1	1	1	1	1	1	1	1	1	1	1	1				1	1	1		
Block diagrams	1	1	1	1	1	1	1	1	1	1	1	1	1	1	1	1	1	1	1	1	1	1	1						1		1
Histograms	1	1	1	1	1	1	1	1	1	1	1	1	1	1	1	1	1	1	1	1	1	1	1	1	1	1	1	1	1		1
Frequency polygons	1	1	1	1	1	1	1	1	1	1	1	1	1	1	1	1	1	1	1	1	1	1	1	1	1	1	1	1	1		1
Pictograms	1	1	1	1	1	1	1	1	1	1	1	1	1	1	1	1	1	1	1	1	1	1	1						1		1
Cumulative frequency	1	1	1	1	1	1	1	1	1	1	1	1	1	1	1	1	1	1	1	1	1	1	1	1	1	1	1	1	1		1
Pie charts	1	1	1	1	1	1	1	1	1	1	1	1	1	1	1	1	1	1	1	1	1	1	1				1	1	1		1
Grouped data	1	1	1	1	1	1	1	1	1	1	1	1	1	1	1	1	1	1	1	1	1	1	1	1	1	1	1	1	1		1
Class intervals	1	1	1	1	1	1	1	1	1	1	1	1	1	1	1	1	1	1	1	1	1	1	1	1	1	1	1	1	1		1
Relative frequency	1	1	1	1	1	1	1	1	1	1	1	1	1	1	1	1	1	1	1	1	1	1	1	1	1	1					1
Median	1	1	1	1	1	1	1	1	1	1	1	1	1	1	1	1	1	1	1	1	1	1	1	1	1	1	1	1	1		1
Mode	1	1	1	1	1	1	1	1	1	1	1	1	1	1	1	1	1	1	1	1	1	1	1	1	1	1	1	1	1		1

Modal class
Arithmetic mean
Geometric mean
Percentiles
Range

Quartiles
Interquartile range
Interpercentile range
Mean deviation

Standard deviation
Time series
Moving averages
Seasonal variation
Trend

Index numbers
Crude rates
Standardized rates
Log paper/scales
Skewness

Probability (discrete)
Addition of probability
Multiplication of
probability
Expected values
Possibility spaces

Mutually exclusive
Exhaustive events
Dependent events
Independent events
Conditional probability

Table 6 Analysis of syllabuses (cont.)

TOPIC	O LEVEL																ADDITIONAL OR ALTERNATIVE O LEVEL														
	Statistics			*Mathematics*													*Statistics*				*Mathematics*										
	A1	S1	W1	L1	L2	A3	J1	J3	ME1	S2	S3	O1	O2	C1	SM1	MM	A2	OC1	C3	L3	A4	J2	L4	OC2	OC3	O3	C2	ME2	S4	SM2	W2
Tree diagrams	1	1	1	1												1															
Scatter diagrams	1	1	1														1	1	1	1	1	1	1				1	1		1	1
Correlation	1	1	1			1											1	1	1	1		1			1		1	1		1	1
Rank correlation	1	1	1			1											1	1	1	1							1	1		1	1
Prod. mmt. correlation			1														1	1	1	1					1			1		1	1
Regression	1	1															1	1			1	1			1						
Regression line (by eye)	1	1															1	1			1	1									
Least squares line																															
Mean of $aX+b$	1		1																1	1	1	1	1		1					1	1
Variance of $aX+b$	1		1																1	1	1	1	1							1	1
Linear transformations	1																1				1	1	1								
Permutations																	1	1	1	1	1	1	1				1	1		1	1
Combinations																	1	1	1	1	1	1	1				1	1		1	1
Discrete probability distributions																1				1	1	1				1					
Uniform distribution																				1						1		1		1	1
Triangular distribution																	1	1	1	1	1	1	1					1			
Binomial distribution	1																1	1	1	1	1	1	1		1	1	1	1		1	1
Means of distributions	1																				1	1	1								
Variances of distributions	1																				1		1								
Density functions																	1	1	1	1	1							1			

Normal curve

Normal tables
Normal binomial
Sum of normal variates
Expectation

Mean and variance
of $aX + bY$
Poisson distribution
Sampling distributions
Probability paper
Standard error of the mean

Null hypothesis
Significance tests
Poisson/binomial
Maximum likelihood
Covariance

Bivariate distributions
Residual variance
Use of t distribution
Use of test
Probability (calculus)

Confidence limits
Normal/Poisson

the industrialization of Europe (History (OC)), design of furniture (Metalwork (S)), growth of giant corporations (History (S)), estimated positions (Navigation (A)) and determination of empirical formulae (Chemistry (A)).

Items which, if taken to a more advanced level, might lead to the use of statistics
Clearly there is no hard dividing line between this and the last section. Most of the previous section could also come under this heading.

There are several items from physics and chemistry – diffusion, Brownian motion, pressure in gases and the gas laws occur in many syllabuses. There is also the spread of epidemics (Human Biology (A), (J)), evolution (Biology (many)), radioactivity (Physical Science (C) and others), dynamic equilibrium of chemical reactions (Physical Chemistry (L)), the effects of temperature, concentration, etc., on reaction rate (Chemistry and Physical Chemistry (L)), the dating of geological materials and events (Geology (S), (L)) and the causes and adjustments of errors (Surveying (A)).

The teacher of statistics in schools who wishes to find new and interesting work for his pupils, could well find what he wants in other syllabuses being taught in the school.

CSE syllabuses

DIFFERENT MODES

The results from four CSE boards were studied for the distribution of candidates entering different modes of the examination. It can be seen from Table 7 that most candidates were entered for Mode I examinations, where the syllabus and examination are controlled by the board. Mode II examinations, set by the board according to a school's chosen syllabus, are fairly uncommon. Mode III, where examinations are set by the school (or a group of schools) on its own syllabus, are gaining in popularity but still form a small percentage of the whole. The West Yorkshire and Lindsey Regional Examining Board is a notable exception. This board is an acknowledged pioneer of Mode III. It will be seen, from the table, that the proportions evident in the all subject entries are repeated in the entries for the mathematics examinations.

Table 7 Percentage entries analysed by mode, for all subjects and mathematics (1977)

BOARD	ALL SUBJECTS			MATHEMATICS		
	Mode I	Mode II	Mode III	Mode I	Mode II	Mode III
Metropolitan Regional Examinations Board*	79·1	5·1	15·8	85·4	0·1	14·5
South Western Examinations Board	83·4	0·8	15·9	83·4	–	16·6
Associated Lancashire Schools Examining Board	81·7	0·7	17·6	80·9	0·3	18·8†
West Yorkshire and Lindsey Regional Examining Board	18·6	9·9	71·6	22·3	11·5	66·2

*The Metropolitan Regional Examinations Board merged with the Middlesex Regional Examining Board in October 1979 to form the London Regional Examining Board.
† Includes Mode III Arithmetic (1583 candidates)

MATHEMATICS MODE I

The fourteen CSE boards offer thirty-four Mode I syllabuses between them, all the boards offering at least two syllabuses. Three boards (Southern Regional Examination Board, Middlesex Regional Examining Board* and East Anglian Examinations Board) also offer a statistics examination in this mode. The statistical content of each of these syllabuses was analysed according to a list of twenty-nine categories. A more detailed list could have been used, but as syllabuses are often not very specific it was decided that a comprehensive, fairly general list would convey a more accurate picture. It was occasionally difficult to classify phrases in a syllabus and sometimes a syllabus was a bit vague. Moreover, a syllabus only provides a basic framework; teachers are free to develop the subject in their own way.

Table 8 shows the statistical content of each syllabus, and the three statistics syllabuses. For comparison in Table 9 we also show the statistical content of four Mode III statistics syllabuses and the syllabus used for the 16+ examination in mathematics offered jointly by Joint Matriculation Board/Associated Lancashire Schools Examining Board/North West

*The Middlesex Regional Examining Board merged with the Metropolitan Regional Examinations Board in October 1979 to form the London Regional Examining Board.

Table 8 Incidence of topics in examination syllabuses

TOPIC	S1	S2	T1	T2	U1	U2	U3	W1	W2	H1	H2	F1	F2	Y1	Y2	Y3	N1	N2
Data collection and tabulation			x*	√				√	x			√	√	√	√	√	√	
Questionnaires			x					√										
Published statistics								√										
Sampling	√	√						√										
Reliability of data								√	√									
Degrees of accuracy				√														
Abuses of statistics			x					√		√								
Pictograms, pie and bar charts	x	x	x	√	√	√	√	√	x	x	√	x	√	√	√	√	√	√
Histograms, frequency polygon	√	√	√	√	√	√	√		√	√	x	√	√	√	√	√		
Comparison of methods																		
Cumulative frequency curves	√	√	√			√			√	√	√	√		√	√	√	√	
Quartiles	√	√							√		√	√		√	√	√	√	
Averages (mean, median, mode)	x	x	x	√	√	√	√	√	x	x	√	√	√	√	√	√	√	√
Inter-quartile range	√	√								√			√		√	√		
Standard deviation			√								√							
Grouped data calculation									√		√		√					
Scattergrams/line fitting				√					√									
Rank correlation				√							√							
Normal curve				√							√							
Prediction of trends													√					
Indices (R P I, etc.)				√														
Time series				√									√					
Probability			x			√	√		x	√	√	√	√		√	√	√	√
Laws of probability						√	√			√	√	√			√	√	√	√
Conditional probability						√	√			√	√		√					
Independence, etc.						√				√	√		√					
Pascal (binomial)						√				√								
Permutations/combinations										√	√	√						
Significance																		
	O†	O	O					O	O	O								

*x indicates topic is in common-core paper where option exists
†O means optional or topic paper containing at least some statistics

TOPIC	A1	A2	A3	A4	K1	K2	L1	L2	L3	M1	M2	G1	G2	G3	E1	E2	MS	SS	AS
SYLLABUS																			
Data collection and tabulation	✓	✓	x		✓	✓	✓	✓	x		x	✓	✓	✓			✓	✓	✓
Questionnaires						✓	✓	x				✓		✓			✓	✓	✓
Published statistics		✓	✓	✓								✓		✓					✓
Sampling	✓		✓	✓		✓	✓	x			✓	✓		✓			✓	✓	✓
Reliability of data	✓		✓		✓					x	✓						✓	✓	
Degrees of accuracy	✓	✓	x		✓	x								✓	x	x			
Abuses of statistics	✓		✓	✓		✓	✓	x			✓		✓	✓	✓		✓	✓	
Pictograms, pie and bar charts	x	✓	x	✓	✓	✓	x	✓	x		x	x	✓	✓	x	x	✓	✓	✓
Histograms, frequency polygon	x	✓	x	✓		✓	✓	✓	x		✓	✓	✓	✓	x	✓	✓	✓	✓
Comparison of methods																✓			
Cumulative frequency curves	✓	✓	✓	✓	✓	✓	✓	✓	x		✓	✓	✓	✓	✓		✓	✓	✓
Quartiles	✓	✓	✓	✓		✓	✓	✓	✓		✓	✓	✓		✓		✓	✓	✓
Averages (mean, median, mode)	✓	✓	✓	✓	✓	✓	✓	✓	x	✓	x	x	✓	✓	x	x	✓	✓	✓
Inter-quartile range	✓	✓	✓	✓		✓	✓	✓	✓		✓	✓	✓	✓			✓	✓	✓
Standard deviation	✓		✓				✓	✓									✓	✓	✓
Grouped data calculation	✓		✓	✓		✓	✓		x		✓	✓					✓	✓	✓
Scattergrams/line fitting	✓	✓	✓	✓		✓	✓	x	✓				✓				✓	✓	✓
Rank correlation	✓																✓	✓	✓
Normal curve	✓	✓						✓							✓	✓	✓	✓	✓
Prediction of trends	✓		✓					✓									✓	✓	✓
Indices (R P I, etc.)	✓		✓														✓	✓	✓
Time series	✓					✓		✓									✓	✓	✓
Probability	✓	✓	✓	✓	✓	✓	✓	✓	x		x	✓	✓	✓	x		✓	✓	✓
Laws of probability	✓	✓			✓	✓								✓			✓	✓	✓
Conditional probability			✓								✓							✓	✓
Independence, etc.	✓	✓																✓	
Pascal (binomial)																		✓	
Permutations/ combinations	✓																		
Significance			✓																
	O		O		O		O			O	O		O			O	O		

Key to syllabuses in Table 8

S1 Mathematics RB ⎱ Southern Regional Examinations Board (these papers have a
S2 Mathematics RC ⎰ common-core paper, also common to Mathematics RA)

T1 Mathematics ⎱
T2 Arithmetic ⎰ South East Regional Examinations Board

U1 Mathematics A ⎫
U2 Mathematics B ⎬ South Western Examinations Board
U3 Arithmetic (Restricted Grade) ⎭

W1 Mathematics ⎱
W2 Arithmetic ⎰ Welsh Joint Education Committee

H1 Mathematics
H2 Elementary Mathematics (Restricted Grade) ⎱ West Midlands Examinations Board

F1 Mathematics 1 ⎱
F2 Mathematics 2 ⎰ West Yorkshire and Lindsey Regional Examining Board

Y1 Mathematics A ⎫
Y2 Mathematics B ⎬ Yorkshire Regional Examinations Board
Y3 Mathematics C (based on SMP) ⎭

N1 Mathematics A ⎱
N2 Mathematics B ⎰ North Regional Examinations Board

A1 Mathematics A (North) ⎫
A2 Mathematics B (North) ⎬ East Anglian Examinations Board
A3 Mathematics A (South) ⎪
A4 Mathematics B (South) ⎭

K1 Mathematics A ⎱
K2 Mathematics B ⎰ Metropolitan Regional Examinations Board*

L1 Mathematics A ⎫
L2 Mathematics B ⎬ Associated Lancashire Schools Examining Board
L3 Mathematics C ⎭

M1 Mathematics A ⎱
M2 Mathematics and Further Maths B ⎰ Middlesex Regional Examining Board*

G1 Mathematics A ⎫
G2 Mathematics B ⎬ North West Regional Examinations Board
G3 Commercial Arithmetic and Statistics ⎭

Regional Examinations Board. Figure 8 shows how often each topic is included in the thirty-seven Mode I syllabuses considered.

There are three types of mathematics syllabus. The traditional syllabuses all contain some statistics. The more modern syllabuses all contain a section on probability and statistics. An increasingly common type of syllabus consists of a common core, invariably containing a fleeting reference to statistics, and a choice of options, one of which either contains a fair proportion of statistics or is wholly on statistics. These are indicated in Table 8 by an 'O' at the foot of the appropriate column.

Each syllabus considered in Table 8 contains some reference to statistics. Averages are also mentioned in each case, though sometimes no further elucidation is given. All but one syllabus mentions the graphical representation of statistical data in simple or detailed form. Probability is included in over 80 per cent of the syllabuses but often only in passing with little elucidation. Cumulative frequency curves and quartiles are a popular topic: easy to teach and examine! The other frequently mentioned topic is the collection and tabulation of data, but perhaps only lip-service is being paid by its inclusion; the closely related topics of the use of published statistics, questionnaires, sampling and the problems of data collection are rarely mentioned.

There are other notable omissions. Only a few boards include correlation. Inference, indices and time-series are frequently ignored, which seems a pity with the current economic interest in the retail price index and its movement. Perhaps the most glaring omission (by two-thirds of the syllabuses) is the absence of any mention of the uses and abuses of statistics. If one teaches statistics at all, a critical evaluation ought to be included.

E1 Mathematics 1 ⎫ East Midland Regional Examinations Board
E2 Mathematics 2 (Restricted Grade) ⎰ (these syllabuses have a common paper)

MS Statistics, Middlesex Regional Examining Board*
SS Statistics R, Southern Regional Examinations Board
AS Statistics, East Anglian Examinations Board

* The Metropolitan Regional Examinations Board merged with the Middlesex Regional Examining Board in October 1979 to form the London Regional Examining Board.

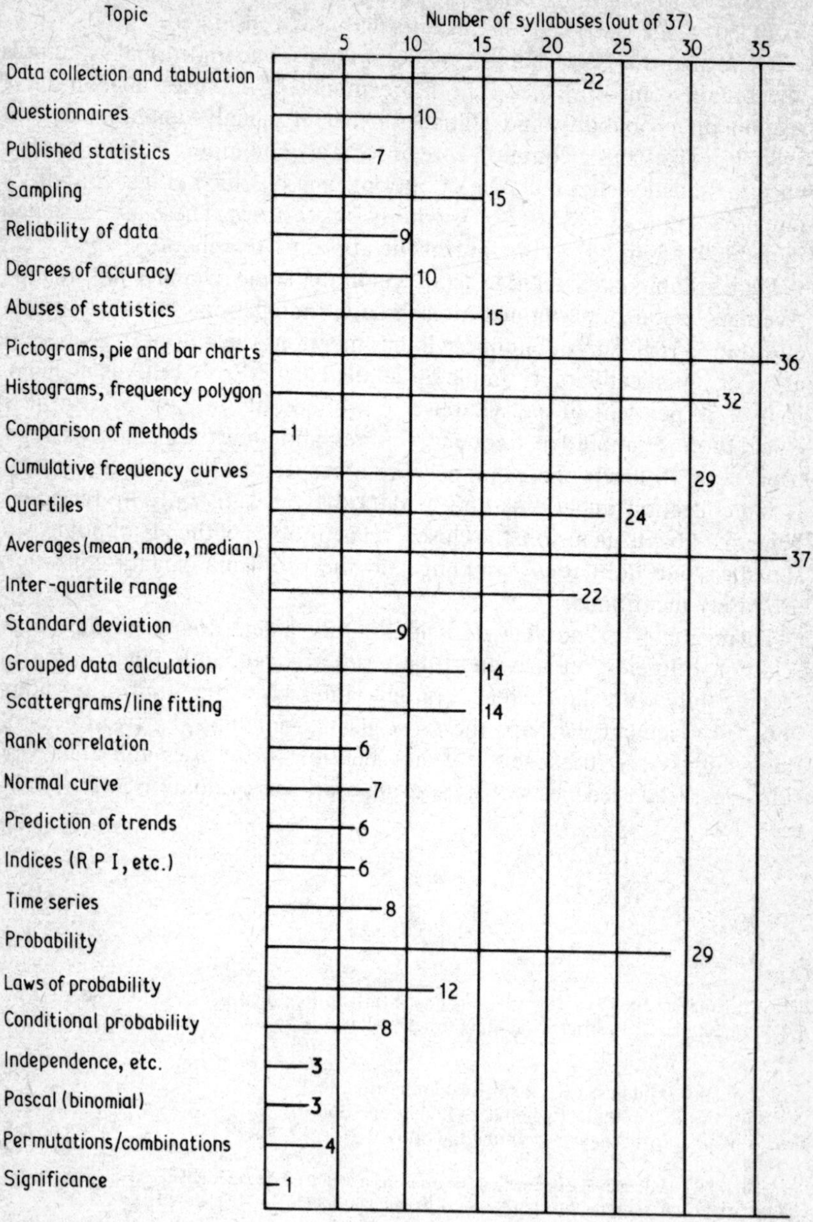

Topic Number of syllabuses (out of 37)

5 10 15 20 25 30 35

Data collection and tabulation — 22
Questionnaires — 10
Published statistics — 7
Sampling — 15
Reliability of data — 9
Degrees of accuracy — 10
Abuses of statistics — 15
Pictograms, pie and bar charts — 36
Histograms, frequency polygon — 32
Comparison of methods — 1
Cumulative frequency curves — 29
Quartiles — 24
Averages (mean, mode, median) — 37
Inter-quartile range — 22
Standard deviation — 9
Grouped data calculation — 14
Scattergrams/line fitting — 14
Rank correlation — 6
Normal curve — 7
Prediction of trends — 6
Indices (R P I, etc.) — 6
Time series — 8
Probability — 29
Laws of probability — 12
Conditional probability — 8
Independence, etc. — 3
Pascal (binomial) — 3
Permutations/combinations — 4
Significance — 1

Fig. 8 Frequency of topics in syllabuses

Table 9 Incidence of topics in four selected examination syllabuses

TOPICS	SYLLABUS 1	2	3	4	x*
Data collection and tabulation	✓	✓	✓	✓	✓
Questionnaires	✓	✓	✓	✓	✓
Published statistics	✓			✓	✓
Sampling	✓	✓	✓	✓	✓
Reliability of data	✓		✓	✓	✓
Degrees of accuracy	✓		✓		
Abuses of statistics	✓	✓		✓	✓
Pictograms, pie and bar charts	✓	✓	✓	✓	✓
Histograms, frequency polygon	✓	✓	✓	✓	✓
Comparison of methods	✓	✓			✓
Cumulative frequency curves	✓	✓	✓	✓	✓
Quartiles	✓	✓	✓	✓	✓
Averages (mean, mode, median)	✓	✓	✓	✓	✓
Inter-quartile range	✓	✓	✓	✓	✓
Standard deviation	✓	✓	✓	✓	✓
Grouped data calculation	✓	✓	✓		✓
Scattergrams/line fitting	✓	✓	✓	✓	✓
Rank correlation		✓	✓		✓
Normal curve		✓	✓	✓	✓
Prediction of trends	✓	✓			
Indices (RPI, etc.)	✓		✓	✓	
Time series	✓		✓	✓	
Probability		✓		✓	✓
Laws of probability					✓
Conditional probability					✓
Independence, etc.					
Pascal (binomial)				✓	✓
Permutations/combinations					
Significance					
					O†

*x is joint 16+ syllabus
†O optional topic paper, 'Choice, Chance and Statistics'

In general it was felt that the statistical content of the CSE Mode I mathematics syllabuses is disappointingly narrow. There is a marked emphasis on the numerical, quantitative side, which is easier to examine; there is not a proper balance with the qualitative aspects of statistics. Though the latter is harder to teach and examine, it is arguably the more important side as, without it, one is faced with the charge that statistics is simply the manipulation of data and as such irrelevant to most people.

MATHEMATICS MODE III

By their very nature it is impossible to generalize about examinations of the Mode III type. The project looked at four CSE Mode III syllabuses in statistics taken by Yorkshire and London schools. The following remarks are based on this small, unrepresentative sample.

As can be seen from Table 9 (which also includes details of the joint 16+ syllabuses referred to earlier) there is a much greater emphasis on the collection, tabulation and interpretation of data together with the limitations. Measures of dispersion, including the standard deviation, as well as measures of spread are included. Correlation is studied and three of the syllabuses include reference to moving and weighted averages. It is interesting to note that two syllabuses contain no probability whatsoever; moreover one studies the 'development and growing importance of statistics as a science'. Another syllabus looks at the distinction between continuous and discrete data. Each syllabus includes some practical work as an integral part of the assessment.

Two schools sent typical examination papers. In general these are closely related to the syllabus with questions requiring critical understanding of techniques. For example, a question asking for a pictograph also asks about the disadvantages of such a diagram. These Mode III syllabuses are to be commended for their wider view of statistics.

TWO SYLLABUSES AND EXAMINATIONS

In this section two typical Mode I Mathematics syllabuses, and the examinations set, are studied in closer detail.

Syllabus A
This consists of a common core and five topics, of which a candidate must select two. In the common core is mentioned: 'Averages, including weighted

averages ... Graphs from statistical data to include pie charts, line and column presentations.' In a recent paper 1 (on this common core) no questions were set on this except for a question on speed; however, this may not be typical.

The statistics syllabus is:

(a) Collection of statistical data
(b) Tabulation
(c) Frequency, cumulative frequency, distribution
(d) Histograms, bar diagrams, straight line graphs, interpretation
(e) Simple average, weighted average
(f) The mean, quartile and standard deviation, by calculation
(g) Median and mode treated graphically

The application of the above to everyday affairs such as the calculation of rates, man-hours worked, income per head, traffic on roads, cricket and football scores, etc.

(h) Measures of dispersion, range and mean deviation
(i) Simple aspects and applications of probability

The first four questions on paper 2 (on the topics) all relied heavily on calculations of varying degrees of difficulty. Two of the questions used purely numerical data, failing to follow the admirably stated emphasis on 'the application of the above to everyday affairs'. Pupils usually cope well with frequency tables, the mode, median and mean; but they find the weighted mean, mean deviation and standard deviation increasingly difficult. The following question on conducting a survey is good, encouraging the pupils to think statistically in formulating their answer:

Imagine you are to conduct a traffic survey to investigate the number, frequency and type of vehicles using a particular road near your school. Describe in detail how you would:

(*i*) obtain the information you require
(*ii*) record and classify this information.

What factors would you need to consider if you wished to obtain information which was representative of typical traffic conditions on this road? In what ways could this survey be of use to anyone else?

Another question was not so good:

Out of a class of 30 children, 20 study statistics, 5 are school prefects and the ratio of boys to girls in the class is 3:2. If one of this class is picked at random, what is the probability that the person picked will be:

(*i*) a girl
(*ii*) a member of the statistics group

(*iii*) a prefect who studies statistics
(*iv*) a boy who is not a prefect?

This question was found to be rather difficult. Presumably candidates were meant to assume that the events 'study statistics', 'are prefects', etc., are independent. Yet nowhere is independence mentioned. It is unfortunate that with these particular figures it is not even possible for the two events to be statistically independent. Questions like this occur frequently; they have more connexion with ratios than with probability.

Syllabus B
This is a more modern approach to the subject. The statistical content is:

Collection and tabulation of statistical material*
Discrete and grouped frequency distributions
Statistical graphs, temperature charts,* block graphs, pie charts*
Frequency polygons and histograms, simple discussions of distribution* and normal distribution*
Mean, mode and median, cumulative frequency, quartiles, range, semi-interquartile range
Permutations and combinations,* e.g., football results, newspaper competitions
Simple ideas of probability.

The content is typical of many of the modern CSE syllabuses, though the section on permutations and combinations sounds quite optimistic for pupils in this ability range (even A-level pupils find it difficult).

The examination contained three questions on the statistics section. None of the topics asterisked was examined in the 1974 papers. One short question was asked for the mean, median and mode. The second question was about faulty boxes of crackers – it asked for a combination of probabilities where independence had to be assumed but was not mentioned. Naturally this can lead to errors. The longer question concerned calculations from grouped data.

Teachers ought not to teach according to examinations yet some, especially the less statistically minded, may be tempted to omit the topics asterisked above; especially as they were also omitted in the 1975 examination. This is a great pity as these topics form a fundamental aspect of statistics. Techniques separated from a basic understanding and appreciation of data make statistics a very dry subject.

OTHER SUBJECTS

The statistical content specifically mentioned in non-mathematical subjects is limited. Statistics is mentioned only in the preamble, rather than in the main body of the syllabus; it occurs most often in geography, but is also mentioned in the area of social/environmental studies. Typical descriptions are: 'the analysis and interpretation of geographical material, e.g., statistics, graphs, diagrams, etc.'; or, in social studies, 'to encourage pupils to develop the skills of using simple statistics'.

The examination papers contain fairly elementary statistical material: reading tables, interpreting bar graphs and pie charts. Project work is increasingly being introduced and there is much scope for statistical work here, though this is naturally left to the discretion of the teacher. Overall there are many opportunities for the strengthening of syllabuses with statistical ideas, but these have yet to be realized.

III. Statistics in mathematics and science courses

Statistics in mathematics courses

This section analyses some of the books used for teaching statistical ideas in mathematics lessons. We begin with a critical appraisal of the statistical content of the two most influential series of mathematical texts, one produced by the School Mathematics Project and the other by the Scottish Mathematics Group, and then review two Schools Council projects. (Statistics texts sometimes used to provide statistical content in mathematics lessons are included in Appendix B.)

THE SCHOOL MATHEMATICS PROJECT[1]

The School Mathematics Project produced Books 1–5 in the 1960s to implement reform of mathematical education. The course was devised with the brighter pupil in mind as it was originally tested in grammar and independent schools, and led to an O-level examination. Books A–H cover a course designed for average pupils wishing to take a CSE examination on one of the 'modern' mathematics syllabuses, while Books X, Y and Z were written to make the transition from Book G to GCE O level. The following comments relate to the 'lettered' books.

Apart from the review chapters, there are eighty-eight chapters and a number of interludes in Books A–H; of these there are three chapters on probability, while statistics has five chapters and two interludes. The main rationale for the statistics course is, according to the authors, to enable pupils to cope with the bombardment of 'so-called statistics from newspapers, advertisement hoardings and television screens'. Moreover, pupils enjoy collecting data of interest to themselves; though this is time-consuming 'the interest and mathematical disciplines involved make it well worthwhile'.

The first chapter on statistics (B9) deals with the collection and presentation of data. The teacher's notes suggest that a class should make a display of good charts from the media, but this is not clarified in the text. For bar charts, important features (such as labelling) are mentioned; pie charts are not labelled with either percentages or degrees, which seems a pity; while for pictograms, an explanation of the key motif is not mentioned in the pupils' text. A number of projects and surveys are suggested. There is a fair spread of questions, including one requiring comparison of methods of representation.

The second chapter (C11) deals with the mode, mean and median. It begins by considering ways of choosing a form representative, by posing the question: what is he/she representing? Here the idea of an average as the representative of a distribution is being put forward. The mode is discussed first. An example showing its limitation leads to the mean. A rather complicated diagram illustrates how the mean is the centre of gravity. The exercises introduce the idea of subtracting a constant to help find the mean and there are questions relating the mean to the total sum. Two disadvantages of the mean form the lead-in to the median, where the even case is dealt with. This is quite a good chapter, though more examples would be useful.

The interlude (Book E) is attractively titled, 'Things are not what they seem'. The importance of (and lack of, in many cases) scales on diagrams is brought out, especially scales not beginning at zero. The care needed over prediction is emphasized (though interpolation is not mentioned). Finally, the confusion caused by columns, areas and heights in pictograms is highlighted. There are some omissions here, such as making predictions from samples, misuse of the mean, choice of sample, and bias. A reference to Darrell Huff's *How to Lie with Statistics*[2] would be valuable in the teacher's notes.

There is a chapter (F7) dealing with calculating the mean of a frequency distribution. The problem surrounding class length is discussed in some detail. An interlude in Book G deals briefly with the distinction between discrete and continuous data, though this is not really used later. There would have been a good opportunity for discussion of errors (inherent or in measurement) here.

Cumulative frequency (G12) is introduced via running totals. This is translated pictorially into a piled-up bar chart to give a hint of the S-shape (ogive). The cumulative frequency tables are written next to the frequency tables such as:

(marks)   81–90   (frequency)   10   (cumulative frequency)   97

which can cause confusion as the last column refers to marks up to 90. The median is estimated both from the frequency table (which seems a bit unnecessary) and the curve. The question is raised whether 20 or 20·5 should be used for plotting the end points of the intervals: as stated in the text it makes little difference to the shape of the curve though it does affect the estimation of the median. The short final chapter (H 5) introduces the inter-quartile range as a measure of spread.

The Books X, Y and Z present little new statistical material. Chapter 10 (Book X) contains a more detailed treatment of inter-quartile ranges and introduces the idea of random selection. There is also an interesting variety of statistical projects suggested in Book X. Some lead to different distributions (normal, Poisson, etc.) while others are experiments concerned with sampling.

The material in these books covers a fair range of statistical ideas though we feel there are serious omissions, which means that a rather narrow view of statistics is presented. In the data collection and representation chapters, little or no mention is made of questionnaires, published statistics, reliability of data and degrees of accuracy. There is nothing on correlation or standard distributions such as the normal curve, which commonly occur in science courses, nor on indices of food prices etc., time series or trend prediction and inference. It would not be possible to include all these topics in the present SMP course, but the selection does result in a rather unbalanced picture of statistics.

Probability (E4) is initally approached via the idea of success fraction in a number of fairly common experiments. Projects are suggested to give the idea of inference from a sample but these are rather open-ended questions, with little guidance offered to the teacher. For example, 'Suppose a firm manufacturing potato peelers wished to know what fraction of its output should be left-handed potato peelers. You have found the fraction of left-handed people in your class. Would this be an accurate enough fraction for the firm to use?'

The rationale given for probability (E7) is that it is a basic foundation for statistics as well as other disciplines; moreover, it is popular with pupils. The equally likely hypothesis is assumed in the approach via set-theory and ratios of corresponding subsets to the whole. Five half-worked examples illustrate the basic result $P(A) = n(A)/n(E)$. The inherent difficulties of listing equally likely outcomes are discussed.

Combined probabilities (for example, of a double six) are discussed by making an exhaustive list of the possible outcomes. This theoretical work is compared with the experimental work done previously. A variety of exercises is presented and pupils are encouraged to display some of their results on bar charts; these are used to bring out the concept of fairness (of coins, spinners, etc.), but variation is not mentioned.

The final chapter on probability (G 3) introduces the multiplication and addition laws of probability intuitively via Venn diagrams; there is a theoretical formulation for the teacher. Combined events are presented in a half-worked example on two dice and one on cards; this is reinforced by the exercises.

The dice example (with sixes) is continued with tree diagrams. The multiplicative property is explained unconvincingly in the pupil text. Pupils find tree diagrams difficult because they are unsure where addition and where multiplication is applicable, and this point is not adequately dealt with, though there is a note for the teacher about the difficulty of combining conditional probabilities. Conditional probability is not mentioned in the pupil texts but is used implicitly in the exercises.

The usual examples of drawing balls from a bag first with replacement and then without replacement are presented. There is a good range of questions including more difficult ones (such as both balls of the same colour, etc.) and three-stage trees. Later questions encourage pupils to draw only the relevant branches of the tree. Some harder, classical problems are given in the teachers' text.

The work on probability is quite good though independence could have been mentioned more overtly. An interesting link with Pascal's triangle has also been ignored. Most importantly, it is unlikely that pupils will see much link between probability and statistics, which was put forward as one of the aims. Perhaps the authors felt that this was, after all, too difficult a topic to include, which seems a pity.

The combined picture of probability and statistics presented by this series is good in parts but limited in its range and balance. Some of the omissions listed are mentioned in the teacher's notes but usually only in passing. For a teacher experienced in statistics such hints are sufficient. But for the average teacher, pressed to complete a syllabus, such guidelines are too easily overlooked. The course is now about ten years old. To have included so much statistics and probability in a school mathematics text must be regarded as a milestone. It is, however, now being revised, and this may well provide an opportunity to give a more balanced view.

SCOTTISH MATHEMATICS GROUP

The Scottish Mathematics Group produced a series of books entitled, *Modern Mathematics for Schools*[3]. The original books were revised in the light of classroom experience, and the second edition published between 1971 and 1975.

Statistics is concentrated into three chapters among the sixty-seven chapters of the first seven books which are 'designed to provide a suitable course for many modern Ordinary level syllabuses in mathematics'. There is also a chapter on probability. All four chapters are in the section headed 'Arithmetic'.

The first chapter (Book 2, 'Arithmetic', Chapter 3) concentrates on the representation of data by pictographs, bar charts, pie charts and line graphs. Collection of data is mentioned in the teacher's notes but hardly referred to in the main text. It is suggested that a class could collect 'newspaper cuttings showing the various pictorial representations of statistics, they might include some particularly good and bad examples'. But the criteria for making the distinction are not given in the text. The relative merits of methods of representation of data are discussed in the teacher's notes but not in the pupils' text: there are no questions on choosing the most appropriate form of representation for a particular set of data. The dangers of trend prediction are mentioned briefly; the way in which a correct representation of facts may nevertheless lead to a false impression from a casual glance is only discussed in a revision exercise.

The next chapter on statistics (Book 4, 'Arithmetic', Chapter 4) lays a solid arithmetical foundation. The example on frequency tables is thoroughly discussed, especially with respect to the choice of class interval. There are plenty of questions on finding the mean, median and mode, but none asking which is most representative in a particular case. The three measures are introduced together with no rationale, while the even case of the median occurs only in the definition. Finally the mean of a simple frequency table (without class intervals) is presented. The connexions with probability and sampling are hardly mentioned in the text, though they are covered more fully in the teacher's notes.

The final chapter on statistics (Book 6, 'Arithmetic', Chapter 2) begins with a revision of the topics already covered. The Σ notation is introduced to calculate the mean of grouped data though strangely pupils find this sign notoriously difficult. The use of an assumed mean is also discussed

– but there is no mention of the introductory technique of subtracting a constant from a group of numbers to simplify calculation. Cumulative frequency tables are written as in the SMP texts. The range and inter-quartile range are hastily introduced before the final example which combines many of the techniques discussed.

The teacher's notes for this chapter mention the need to remind pupils of the dangers arising from the unthinking use of statistics, and also refer to the use of published statistics and sampling methods, though regrettably these are not referred to in the pupils' notes. As a whole this chapter provides a thorough foundation for examination topics, though it does seem a bit hurried.

The omission of index numbers from the standard texts has been remedied in one of the four chapters of a supplementary booklet. Very little explanation of the reasons for, or the uses of, index numbers is given, though there are exercises in calculating index numbers, using index numbers to find actual values and changing the base year.

The chapter on probability opens with many new concepts and talks of probability as 'the "limit" of the relative frequencies of the outcome in large numbers of trials', which seems rather complicated phrasing. Standard experiments on dice, beads and coins are suggested before moving on to the theory which is based on the equally likely hypothesis. There is a good selection of exercises, ending with a slight hint of conditional probability. Expected frequency is introduced next but without mentioning independence – this loses a good opportunity for discussion and gaining insight. Mutually exclusive events are approached by listing, with experiments such as getting a double six or a score of seven; visual arrays are used. One feels that in this chapter a number of rather sophisticated topics have been introduced at a somewhat superficial level, glossing over difficulties. Much would depend on the teacher.

The gap between the teacher's notes and the pupils' text is particularly important in a series aimed at mixed-ability groups. In much of the work questions are set at three different levels, presumably to permit a pupil to work at his own pace. Thus it is important for explanations to be contained in the pupils' text.

These books provide a fairly solid and thorough foundation which may help pupils in passing examinations. The main body of many modern syllabuses has been covered. The supposed frills have been scrupulously omitted, and this is where one feels the disappointment. There is little imagination in the preparation of the statistical material, and one wonders how many of these concepts can be expected to survive beyond the examination stage.

MATHEMATICS FOR THE MAJORITY[4]

This Schools Council project (1967–72) produced fourteen teacher's guides for work with pupils of average and below average ability aged 13–16. The continuation project (1971–75) developed pupil material. It is suggested by the projects that formal class teaching should be minimal and that pupils should learn mathematics through practical and individual work in real-life situations, with the teacher in the role of adviser/tutor.

The guide on probability and statistics is entitled *Luck and Judgement*. The practical work consists of thirty-two activities connected with dice, birthdays, coins, cards, beads, letter frequency, lengths, and football. It is suggested that only brief instructions should be given, leaving the details of presentation and interpretation to emerge from discussion. There is an appendix on the presentation of instructions to pupils: an experiment is developed as **a** a workcard, **b** a duplicated worksheet with more detailed instructions and, interestingly, **c** a tape.

Two longish chapters analyse the activities according to their common features. First a priori situations are analysed and then a posteriori situations (such as distributions and samples). The approach is that, after exploring real events and looking for patterns in the results, pupils should try to find theoretical explanations. The discussion of probabilistic situations (coins, dice, etc.) is fairly standard. More interesting is the analysis of other situations, such as the record of school attendance or of goals in football. This chapter presents a useful discussion of some neglected though important areas of statistics, though there is little on estimation and bias.

For questionnaires, rather than a list of dos and don'ts, it is suggested that pupils be given test runs. The section on sampling deals only with early qualitative ideas. There are also chapters on theoretical probability, averages, dispersion and correlation. These latter topics are rather hastily covered but the book can be recommended.

The continuation project developed packs containing workcards, background booklets, teacher's guides, photographs and drawings, models, tapes and games and puzzles. We examined five[4] of them. On the whole the statistical content seems rather limited. There are complications in real-life situations, which make the mathematics rather difficult, and many situations considered seem somewhat contrived. It also requires a certain level of sophistication to extract the essentials from a common situation. Simplifications such as frictionless pulleys and weightless strings have their advantages!

For example, pupils are asked to decide, from a list of nine answers, the most appropriate solutions to six urban problems. The teacher's guide states that the possible arrangements of solutions can lead to work on probability and methods of enumeration. It is surely more useful for pupils to discuss the possible solutions and the place of statistics in their reasoning than to follow on with work on probability in this artificial way. In another assignment, workcards showing pupils how to construct a pin-ball machine and a one-armed bandit also ask pupils to decide pay-outs. Naturally trial-and-error provides the basic grounding, but no help is given, even in the teacher's guide, on how to proceed further: this involves the difficult notion of expected values. The same idea is also involved in an assignment on light bulbs which contains rather difficult questions.

Among the various examples of sampling there is no discussion of bias or estimation of population parameters. Much of the work is fairly obvious such as drawing pie charts for television programmes or bar charts on travel to school. This would be acceptable in a coherent programme of work, but the packs seem rather disjointed in their statistical approach. Moreover some of the language is rather sophisticated, for the majority of pupils.

Statistics in science courses

This section looks at some of the texts and materials commonly used in science teaching with the 11–16 age-group, to see what use is made of statistics and statistical techniques. Particular attention has been paid to texts which adopt the newer thematic and integrated approach to the teaching of science.

The most influential materials in this field have been those produced by projects financed by the Nuffield Foundation. The specialist Nuffield Biology, Nuffield Chemistry and Nuffield Physics were first published in 1966 and 1967. These were followed in the early 1970s by the Nuffield Combined Science and Nuffield Secondary Science projects. More recently there have been the Schools Council Integrated Science Project (SCISP), Schools Council Project Technology and the Schools Council Science 5–13 project. An even more recent arrival on the scene is the Scottish *Science for the 70s* by A. J. Mee, P. Boyd and D. Ritchie.

In a 1973 survey (and hence too early to measure accurately the impact of the more recent projects in schools) Booth[5] reports about one-third of secondary schools using the specialist Nuffield material and about a quarter using Nuffield Secondary Science and Combined Science with the appropriate age-groups. Only ten per cent were not using materials from at least one of the Nuffield or the three Schools Council projects. Further evidence on the use being made of these materials can be found in Tebbutt[6] and Nicodemus[7].

Since the philosophy and much of the content of the early specialist Nuffield guides is incorporated in the more recent Combined Science and Secondary Science projects, this section concentrates on these last two projects as being representative of 'Nuffield' work and thinking. Other sections consider the Schools Council Science 5–13 and Integrated Science projects. The Scottish 'Science for the 70s' course is considered since it is a new course which is becoming very popular in the 11–13 age-range. (A quick read of the Schools Council Project Technology material indicated that no great use was made of statistical ideas.)

SCIENCE 5 TO 13[8]

This project was sponsored jointly by the Schools Council, the Nuffield Foundation and the Scottish Education Department. The material consists of twenty-seven guides to teachers giving details of experiments and investigations that may be done, together with reproductions of some children's work to show what might be expected. A close inspection was made of the six volumes entitled *Using the Environment*, since this promised to be the richest source of sampling and statistical work arising from investigations. This was supplemented by considering three of the other guides *Children and Plastics* (stages 1 and 2), *Coloured Things* (stages 1 and 2) and *Change* (stage 3). References to these guides will be given as UE 1, 2.1, 2.2, 3.1, 3.2 and 4, CP, CT and C respectively.

The work is designed for children aged 5 to 13. The three stages referred to in the guide titles are stages in the Piagetian sense of children's mental development. Stage 1 is the transition from intuition to concrete operations and the early stages of concrete operations; stage 2 is the later stage of concrete operations; and stage 3 is the transition to abstract thinking. In terms of our 11–16 project, the stage 2 and stage 3 material is most relevant.

The emphasis of the scheme is on practical investigations by the children who will therefore produce a lot of data. The variability inherent in this data is consistently underplayed. We have, for instance, one set of results using elastic bands leading to Hooke's law where the instruction is to draw a straight line (U E 2.1, p. 76); the force required to pull up different aged broad bean seeds from soil also has to give a straight-line graph (U E 3.1, p. 34). An experiment for finding the mean of dissolved material in 200 cm³ of different types of water uses only one sample of each type of water (C, p. 59).

The guides seem to assume that the pupils are already familiar with statistical concepts and techniques, and require quite a sophisticated understanding of data presentation techniques.

Techniques and concepts used

As well as many examples of tabulated data the following are included:

1 Tallying – number of vehicles in quarter hours (U E 1, Ch. 3, and implicitly in many other places).

2 Block graphs and bar charts with nominal, ordinal, linear and ratio scales and with scales used on the vertical axis – drying times for different materials (U E 1, p. 17); animals found in one hour by size and depth of digging (U E 2.1, p. 15); classification and amounts of different types of litter collected in fifteen minutes (U E 2.1, p. 82); rainfall and temperature (U E 2.2, p. 20); number of seeds germinating U E 2.2, p. 24); wind direction and bird numbers (U E 2.2, p. 87); contents of packets of 'Swoop' (U E 2.2, p. 91); seeds in pods (U E 3.1, p. 66); number of fruits attached to wings on branch of a lime tree (U E 3.1, p. 70); weed frequency on mown or rough grassland (U E 3.2, p. 23); stretching plastic strips (CP, p. 38); colour of cars, year produced, popular cars (CT, p. 35); a brightness scale (CT, p. 36); plant growth on and around tree stumps (U E 3.2, p. 17).

3 Frequency polygons and charts based on time series – timing animals through mazes (U E 2.1, p. 60); height of plants for time of growth (U E 2.2, p. 31); duck weed leaves and numbers of *Daphnia* (water fleas) over a period of weeks (U E 2.2, p. 41); time taken to slide down a slope (U E 2.2, p. 65); cooling 'curves' for different insulators (C P, p. 19).

4 Variability is often implicit, as in many of the above examples, and in the landing position of ash and sycamore seeds from given height (U E 3.1, p. 54). It is considered explicitly in U E 3.1 (pp. 64ff) where there is a list of items which may show variability in qualitative or quantitative ways. This work is linked to the idea of a distribution

though the distinction between sampling and population distributions is not drawn. 'Normal' is used in the sense of 'usual', and there is some rather odd curve-fitting to distributions with discrete data.

5 Two-way classification tables – popularity of food stuffs for birds over types of bird (UE 2.2, p. 92); different insects on different flowers (UE 3.1, p. 19).

6 Sampling is discussed specifically in UE 3.2 (pp. 20ff). The use of a sample to predict the whole is illustrated by referring to testing a baby's bath water, putting a knife in a fruit cake to see if it is cooked, testing drinking water, and Gallup polls. A simulated sample from spatial distributions of plants which are mixed, clustered or separate shows some of the problems that may arise. The use of random numbers for sampling from land areas is also discussed. Sampling is used as a basis for estimating the number of daisies on a lawn and conkers on a tree (UE 2.1, p. 26). There is also a reference to a sampling distribution of the position of birds seen on a housing estate (UE 2.2, p. 88), a comparison between two samples is made in UE 3.1 (p. 71) between a hundred leaves of 'rat's-tail' plantain leaves from trampled mown grassland and shady well-vegetated land.

7 Averages are used for the average time from laying to hatching of eggs laid by a cabbage white butterfly (UE 2.2, p. 34); the average of three times for sliding down a slope (UE 2.2, p. 65); average landing positions of ash and sycamore seeds (UE 3.1, p. 54).

8 Correlation is mentioned by name when comparing the number of gulls observed with the air temperature (UE 2.2, p. 87); negative correlation is mentioned in connexion with the distribution of aquatic animals found compared with depth of lake water (UE 3.2, p. 5). In neither case is there any calculation involved.

Experiments which lead or could lead to more sophisticated statistical procedures

1 UE 2.1, p. 64 has what could be a sophisticated investigation into the eating habits of different types of caterpillar with a comparison of their weights.

2 The growth of numbers of *Daphnia* (water fleas) over a period of weeks (UE 2.2, p. 41) leads to the problem of predicting future numbers.

3 The question, 'Would a smaller animal become a skeleton more rapidly?' (UE 2.2, p. 56) raises many interesting statistical possibilities.

4 'Do birds select particular things from the constituents of commercial

wild bird food?' is an experiment based on 'Swoop' (UE 2.2, p. 91). This is generalized later to the popularity of various foodstuffs, the type of day and the height at which the food is placed – a real multivariate problem.

5 The problems of population, overcrowding and competition for animals and plants are raised in UE 3.1 (p. 12).

Summary
The statistical knowledge implied by the Science 5–13 course is considerable. Since very few of the techniques are actually taught within the course proper, this must be done by the teacher or in some other part of the school curriculum. The present mathematics courses and syllabuses would cover some of the ideas but not all – particularly not by the time they are needed in this course.

'SCIENCE FOR THE SEVENTIES'[9]

This Scottish series, by A. J. Mee, *et al.*, consists of two pupils' textbooks and two teachers' guides. Designed for use with children aged 12–14 in Scotland, the authors suggest that it can be used with 11–14 mixed-ability classes in England.

The course describes a series of experiments for pupils. The references in the following analysis are to the numbers of the experiment. Pupils are expected to be able to interpret simple tabulated data, block graphs and bar charts. As in Science 5–13 the nature and extent of variability is understated and many statistical ideas are implicit rather than explicit in the experiments. When the emphasis is qualitative or on the founding of scientific rather than statistical principles this is acceptable. In other cases, when variability is an essential part of the problem, it is not – as, for instance, in answering, 'What is a child's lung capacity?' (1.24), and judging distances using only one eye (11.10).

Occasionally statistical ideas are mentioned specifically. Paragraph 1.17 on living things talks about variability of pulse rate. Experiment 1.35 collects various types of data from the children – height, eye colour, hair colour, ability to roll tongue, hand-span, pulse, left- or right-handed – which cannot fail to raise difficulties of classification and measurement, which is all to the good. A reference to the likely hair colour of a future husband for the girls raises too many problems about the difference between the sample and the appropriate population to be a good example of probability. For this section the teacher's notes refer to the normal distribution of heights of first-years, and ask the teacher to explain in simple terms the characteristics of a normal distribution, but they do not spell out what the characteristics are. A block graph is wrongly called a histogram and there is a very misleading comment on eye colour, hair colour, and the normal distribution. In 5.3 the distribution of speeds of particles (molecules) is said to be normal and a normal curve is drawn. There has been no build up for children to be able to interpret such a probability density function, and the whole concept is probably far too sophisticated for children of this age.

Specific statistical techniques are also required in experiments 6.16, 12.3, 12.24 and paragraphs 14.7 and 14.10. Experiment 6.16 is on recording the rate of heart-beat of a chicken embryo as the temperature is changed. The graph given is a combination of a bar chart and a frequency polygon and is not particularly easy to follow. A more standard scattergram might have led more clearly to the ideas of regression involved. In 12.3 pupils are asked to find the densities of a number of different rocks and say how the average result compares with that of the earth's crust. There is, of course, no reason why there should be any connexion between these two numbers. The sample of rocks was chosen for its geological interest, not to represent the density of the earth's crust. Experiment 12.24 has children finding the amount of moisture in a sample of soil. They are then asked to compare their results with those obtained by other groups. The nature and basis of such comparison is not clear even in the teacher's guide. The problem of fluoridation of water and its effect on dental decay is considered in paragraphs 14.7 and 14.10. Paragraph 14.7 asks the pupils to find the number of teeth with fillings in their class and compare with another class and with a quoted national picture of 2/100. Again the nature of the comparison to be made and the effect of sampling error are not mentioned even in the teacher's guide. The effect of sampling error is again ignored in 14.10, where the distributions of numbers of teeth with fillings of 500 people from town A and 527 from town B are given. The pupils are asked to conclude that the fluoridation in town A gives better teeth than in town B on a very flimsy basis. From the statistical point of view this course is very disappointing. It does not make use of statistical ideas inherent in the experiments, and makes too many errors when it does try to go further.

NUFFIELD COMBINED SCIENCE[10]

Nuffield Combined Science is a course for 11- to 13-year-old children. It consists of two activities packs for children, three Teacher's Guides and a number of film loops. It is not so practically oriented as Science 5–13 and involves more formal exercise work. In the following analysis 1(45) refers to activity number 45 in activity pack book 1; 1.45 refers to page 45 of Teacher's Guide 1.

Overall the statistical content of the course is good. There is a very early introduction to the idea of variability in sections 1(62) to 1(66) (1.45ff.) in a section entitled, 'Statistics'. Activities in this section include the 'best' value for ten readings of a mass; the average number of words in three lines of print and what to do with part lines if used to estimate the number of words in longer passages; shoe sizes; and measuring lengths. There are some interesting and unusual statistical concepts touched on in these experiments. Problems of classification are exemplified by asking if see-saw is one or two words; accuracy and the nature of data, by asking if 7·3 is an appropriate mean number of words per line since we can't have 0·3 of a word; sample to population and back to sample, by using the shoe-size data to advise a shopkeeper how many pairs of shoes of each size to stock; outliers and their effect on accuracy of averages, by giving five children's measurement of the same length as 50·4, 50·5, 50·2, 44·2 and 50·4. There is also a formal section for teachers (3.233ff.) giving concise notes on collection of data and types of data; recording and plotting, interpretation ('We must be careful that even if the ideas the children derive from this experiment are primitive, there should be none that they have to unlearn later when perhaps statistics is studied in its own right'); histograms with a brief mention of the normal curve; and mean, median and mode. Teacher's guide 1.28 also brings up the problems of a complete census, even in something as seemingly simple as attendance at a garden fête.

There are some items which start well but either go wrong or give insufficient help, such as, 'A tree is twice as high if its trunk is twice as thick. Is this true?' 2(87). On measuring the growth of seedlings, the teacher is told in 1.187 to remove early and late sprouters, with no indication of the implication of this for the results. And we still have springs stretching to give (exact) straight-line graphs (2(33)), and measuring the amount you breathe done once only 4(27).

There are some good experiments from the statistical point of view. There are pieces of experimental design in 7(27) when considering the effect of different concentrations of disinfectant on bacteria; in 7(16) on 'Are there microbes on your fingers whether clean, dirty, washed and dried with a clean or dirty towel?'; and the effect of different factors on total and average heights of ten growing seedlings 2(78). A comparison of relative proportions of body sizes for babies, children and adults has the added question, 'Is it fair to make measurements like these on only one baby and one adult?' 2(83). An eight-sided spinner is used to simulate two-dimensional particle movement in 7(45) to give some indication of diffusion.

Finally we quote a few comments from the teacher's guide which show a sound attitude to statistics: 'samples must be representative' (1.45); 'the method of sampling and the reliability of the numerical result can be discussed' (within the context of estimating the number of earthworms in an area such as a football pitch) (1.71); 'we want children to realize that their inferences are based on several experiments' (1.166); 'density – another chance to realize the value of averaging a number of results rather than relying on one' (1.274).

NUFFIELD SECONDARY SCIENCE[11]

This course is designed for pupils aged 13 to 16 who are unlikely to take O level. A thematic approach to the teaching of science is adopted. There is a teacher's guide, and eight pupil books are under the general title *Themes*. Chapters take the form of 'fields' within the themes. References in the following analysis are given by volume number and field, so 1.34 is field 34 in theme 1. The teacher's guide has a section on aims of secondary science. Some of these relate to statistics:

The investigatory approach should stimulate the pupils' ability to ... suggest solutions from reliable and comprehensive data ... they should be aware of the accuracy of the data used, the magnitude of errors inherent in the work ... work is included [to] help pupils recognize errors and the ways in which data may be distorted for commercial and propaganda purposes and to be alert to such practices as poor sampling techniques and unwarranted extrapolations. The ability to appraise data and evidence of all kinds is valuable and one which we should certainly try to develop in our pupils.

And in the introduction to *Theme 1*:

To be more confident in the results it is necessary to repeat the experiment many times. The ideas involved in thinking about the size of a reliable sample could perhaps be followed up in a mathematics lesson.

This is fine and encouraging, and with a knowledgeable and statistically well qualified teacher there are many openings in the course. For less well qualified teachers the books raise very interesting problems but do not give sufficient help in indicating what statistical techniques and concepts may be found helpful in pursuing the investigations thoroughly and enabling the pupil to make a sound criticism of his findings. In the eight themes there are a large number of investigations involving statistical ideas. The references in the following should be taken as representative rather than exhaustive.

Classification of data and the different types of data that can arise are two ideas that are continually being met. Variability underlies much of the work though sometimes it is used as in 7.24, 'These voltage results are not always exactly reproduceable', and sometimes explained away as in 6.12 on acceleration, 'If, however, the exact quantitative relationship does not emerge...'! Sampling is also a prevalent theme, but 1.12, 'The square metre to be surveyed is selected by throwing a peg at random', for using quadrats in a field, could be misleading. Averages are also used widely, not only as a summary measure but also to gain accuracy as in 6.14, in timing the fall of small balls through liquid paraffin four times, and 6.17 on timing vibrations of a hack-saw blade. Continually pupils have to read data in such diverse examples as: 1.23 on crops raised in air or air enriched with CO_2; 2.23 butter-fat from cows of different ancestry; 3.12 figures on smoking and health; 5.32 lighting values required for different work and premises; 6.14 cars and lorries in America; 7.33 the world's producers and consumers of oil; 7.56 sources and size of radiation. Pupils' own data have to be displayed as bar charts, histograms, pie charts and frequency polygons.

There is also much work that gives an early introduction to more sophisticated statistical ideas. Although not mentioned explicitly, the frequent use of a control leads to many paired comparisons involving the significance of results as in: 1.23 does a CO_2 enriched atmosphere help plant growth?; 3.18 does increased water consumption lead to increased urination?; 1.21 do some animals move to damp areas and some to dry areas?; 2.11 is hoeing an efficient method of controlling leaves?; 2.21 breeding mini-mice and mighty mice; 2.23 the effect of genetic selection on resistance of rats' teeth to bacterial decay and on the oil content of maize plants; 2.26 progeny testing of bulls to become AI donors; 3.41 distinguishing butter from margarine. All these involve ideas of significance and are studied statistically rather than scientifically.

Regression is implied in: 1.31 does the dry mass of plants increase at a steady rate as they grow?; 3.43 speed of spelling and drawing increases with practice; 6.14 stopping distance of a bicycle travelling at different speeds; 8.12 radius of satellite orbit compared to time of revolution; 2.26 effect on egg laying of selective breeding of hens; 2.34 herring landings 1903–49 and spread of collared doves – distance from Tenby compared with time since first sighting in 1547.

Multivariate and experimental design problems are raised by: 1.31 on the effect of fertilizers on plant growth and the effect of watering on growth of lawns; and 1.32 on the effects of temperature, food and alcohol on the growth of yeast cells.

Extrapolation is used in: 1.23 is there a limit to the world population which could be fed?; and 7.39 when will our fuel be used up?

Early ventures into the realm of decision theory are involved in: 2.13 on why did the farmer kill the sow when he did?; and 7.36 on the size of gas-holders needed to cope with seasonal fluctuating demands for gas.

Bivariate data and their representation are in: 3.14 pulse rate compared to fitness training; 2.24 do tall parents have tall children? 2.34 on pairs of nesting robins compared with coldness in the previous winter also involves the idea of correlation.

Probability is raised by problems of order and disorder in 4.43 on general entropy problems and conditional probability is implied in the table of 2.39 on the probability of a second child suffering from some genetic defect in the same family.

Three sections use data in a substantial way. These are 2.39 man's effect on evolution; 3.44 studying human behaviour; and 3.5 man in the world. In these sections there are data on estimated populations of the blue whale, the number of factory ships at sea, erythromycin resistance, animals killed in the 1967/68 foot-and-mouth epidemic, sufferers from diabetes, smoking, alcohol consumption and fox-hunting. There are problems on making food production more efficient, fluoridation of water, dams and reservoirs, and pollution. There are examples referring to opinion polls, the use of electricity, transport journeys, school dinners, insurance, marriages, numbers of children and market research.

All in all the course provides a statistical feast, but there is insufficient help given for the less well qualified teacher.

SCHOOLS COUNCIL INTEGRATED SCIENCE PROJECT (SCISP)[12]

This project followed on from the Nuffield Combined Science and the Nuffield Secondary Science projects and has a similar philosophy. The material is in four parts all with the general title *Patterns*. The material is for the older and more able pupils in the 11–16 age-range, leading to GCE O level. Of the courses studied, it makes the widest use of data and statistical ideas. A great concern is shown for the impact of science on society and the environment, hence many of the ideas studied are very similar to ideas studied in the social sciences and economics. The text in the pupils' manuals is divided into a number of investigations referred to in the following analysis – for example 1.2.19 is the nineteenth investigation in the book *Patterns 1*, Chapter 2. Most of the questions asked about data are on a relatively simple level of interpretation. Some of the more sophisticated approaches are reproduced below.

As an indication of the social science/economics emphasis of the course consider the following sections: 1.2.8 on the turnover of commodity prices on the London Metal Exchange; 1.3.5 on opinion polls and sample surveys; 1.3.6 on population pyramids for different times with questions asking pupils to discuss the social consequences; 1.3.7 on the population of England and Wales since 100 000 BC, with work on prediction of future population size; 1.4.8 on questionnaire design with an example using contrived questions to get different answers; 1.6.13 on UK consumers' expenditure on food for 1959–69 (what do the figures reveal about the popularity of quick frozen foods?); 1.8.20 on fertilizer use compared with grain yield for various countries (what pattern does it clearly indicate?); 2.11.9 on percentage of households owning different electrical appliances in various countries, and the percentage of growth of UK owners of food/drink mixers; 2.11.15 on the number of exchange connexions and telephones in UK 1920–72 with predictions to 1980; 2.12.11 on the Lynmouth flood; 2.13.8 on land, water and air speed records 1898–1967 and the cost of Concorde; 2.14.2 on socio-economic class, change of categories 1931–61 and the distribution of personal incomes in UK 1966 (illustrated by a very poor graph); 2.15.5 on a survey of country of origin, living conditions and family size, etc. for the pupil's local area (with not much practical help in either pupil or teacher notes); 3.2.26 figures on smoking and lung cancer; 3.5.1 on the cost of different means of obtaining energy; 4.1.3 includes the bill of mortality for the plague year 1665; UK certified sickness 1954–67, annual mortality rates for tuberculosis, scarlet fever, smallpox, whooping cough, measles and diphtheria 1851–1966; 4.2.10 is an attitude survey to indicate personality; 4.6.22 includes figures for diabetes in Great Britain; and 4.10.1 birth rate, death rates, and predictions compared with actual figures.

In the more generally accepted fields of school science we have very similar ideas occurring as in Nuffield Secondary Science. There are similar blind spots, with elastic strings giving an exact straight-line graph (1.1.9). Occasionally statistics are not used when they could be illuminating, as in insurance problems (2.12.12), or in attempted suicide rates in cities (2.9.3), but this is rare. Many and various types of data have to be interpreted with 1.8.19 on ion concentration in four lakes, 2.9.1 on population size of two competing species, 3.4.10 on insecticide residue in terrestrial or aquatic birds, as well as the many examples mentioned above. The use of a sample to make deductions about the population occurs in 1.3.5 on estimating school population, dandelion population on a lawn and organisms in a mini-pond. Predictions from data, implications of data and questions on the scientific consequences of data occur in 3.1.20 on the effects of pumping liquid waste into well and local earthquake shocks near Denver, Colorado; 3.2.4 on percentage of total power by man or machine in UK 1850–1970; 3.4.1 on consumption, use and reserves of coal, oil and gas; 4.6.18 on number of haemophiliacs; and in many other places. Regression and time series data are used in 1.4.6 on mass of penguins compared with temperature range of habitat; 1.4.7 on variation of height of pupils in the same year group; 2.10.12 consumption of sulphur and other materials used for sulphuric acid manufacture 1959–68; 3.4.4 on coronary heart disease in males compared with consumption of sugar; 4.2.5 on the effect of learning on the speed of drawing a simple figure. Comparisons of samples which call for some elementary ideas about significance occur in 1.8.21 on the effect of fluoridation on tooth decay; 4.6.5 on the effect of selection on amount of oil in corn kernel and on the resistance of rats' teeth to decay; and 4.6.8 on the development of resistance by bacteria to erythromycin. Variability occurs in many places but particularly in the teacher's guide to 2.9 on biological populations. There is also a glancing reference to variability in 3.1.5 where 'force × distance remains the same, or nearly the same'. Work using simulations is in 4.6.11 where coloured beads are used to simulate genetic inheritance; 4.6.20 where again beads simulate the Hardy–Weinberg law; and 4.8.10 where radioactive decay is modelled by dice throwing.

Potentially the most far-reaching statistical section is 4.7.22. Here the pupil is given data on cars and motor cycles in Great Britain; casualties suffered by different types of road user; the growth of traffic; the trend away from the railways; public transport data; Road Research Laboratory report on the effect of water, tread on tyres, fog, age of driver, alcohol and speed on driving standards; with some ideas of costs of road improvements, and international variation on deaths of car occupants. With all this data, and little other guidance, the pupil is asked to imagine he is Minister of Transport and find the most effective approach to reducing road accidents within a limited budget. Wow!!

CONCLUSION

This survey of some of the texts more widely used in the teaching of science has revealed much less overlap of specific examples and experiments used than might have been expected. Texts for younger children rightly concentrate on developing fundamental scientific ideas and play down the role of variability, and hence of statistics. Texts for the older children reveal a growing use and appreciation of the role of statistics in science. There is also work which implies some intuitive understanding of statistical inference and some appreciation of the place of statistics in decision-making.

We have spelt out many of the detailed experiments involving statistical ideas so that those teaching statistics will realize that the examples are many and various. They are not confined to genetics in biology and error analysis in physics. Probability is the one notable exception in the texts covered. Very little reference is formally made anywhere to probability – though clearly all statistical inference implies some appreciation of its nature.

References and notes

1. School Mathematics Project (SMP), Books 1–5, Cambridge University Press, 1965–72. Books A–H, X, Y, Z. Cambridge University Press, 1968–74.
2. DARRELL HUFF, *How to Lie with Statistics*. Gollancz, 1954; Penguin Books, Harmondsworth, 1973.
3. Scottish Mathematics Group, *Modern Mathematics for Schools*. Blackie, Glasgow and Chambers, Edinburgh, 2nd edn, 1971–75.

4. The teacher's guides are published by Hart-Davis Educational, St Albans. *Luck and Judgement*, the guide on probability and statistics, was published in 1971. The Statistical Educational Project team looked at five of the pupil packs produced by the Mathematics for the Majority Continuation Project. Four packs have been published by Schofield & Sims, Huddersfield: *Buildings* (1974), *Communication* (1974), *Travel* (1975) and *Physical Recreation* (1975).

5. N. BOOTH, 'The impact of science teaching projects on secondary education', *Education in Science*, **63**, 1975, 27–30.

6. M. J. TEBBUTT, 'The impact of curriculum developments', *Education in Science*, **67**, 1976, 20–1.

7. R. B. NICODEMUS, 'Discrepancies in measuring adoption of new curriculum projects', *Education in Science*, **65**, 1975, 26–8.

8. The twenty-seven teacher's guides are published by Macdonald Educational. The six volumes entitled *Using the Environment* are: 1. *Early Explorations* (1974); 2. *Investigations*, Parts 1 and 2 (1974); 3. *Tackling Problems*, Parts 1 and 2 (1974); 4. *Ways and Means* (1975). The other guides discussed are: *Coloured Things*, stages 1 and 2, and *Change*, stage 3 (1973); *Children and Plastics*, stages 1 and 2 (1974).

9. A. J. MEE, P. BOYD and D. RITCHIE, *Science for the Seventies*. Heinemann Educational Books, 1971–73.

10. Nuffield Combined Science, *Activities Pack* 1 and 2. Longman 1970; reprinted, 1977. *Teacher's Guide* 1, 2 and 3. Longman, 1970, 1971, 1970.

11. Nuffield Secondary Science, *Themes 1–8* and *Themes 1–8: Teacher's Guide*. Longman, 1971.

12. Materials from the Schools Council Integrated Science Project (13–16) are published by Longman and Penguin Education, Harmondsworth. Each of the four parts includes a pupils' manual, teacher's guide, technician's manual and topic books. The pupils' manuals discussed are: Patterns 1, *Building Blocks* (1973), Patterns 2, *Interactions and Building Blocks* (1973), Patterns 3, *Energy* (1974), Patterns 4, *Interactions and Change* (1974).

IV. Statistics in humanities and social science courses

In this chapter three subjects are considered in detail: geography, history and economics. Geography and history reach most pupils in some form or other, though not necessarily taught in the manner described here, which makes use of statistical presentation. Economics includes some statistical material for almost all learners, with considerably more for those following some more recent courses. Evidence from the examining boards and from our own survey suggests that this subject is offered in most sixth forms, and that about 10 per cent of O-level candidates take economics. Rather more than this, about one in six, are thought to be receiving economics tuition before the age of 15, when non-examination classes are taken into account.

In the second part of the chapter brief comments are given on subjects which, though widely taught, generally provide minimal statistical content, and on those which, though of considerable potential statistical interest, appear to reach (at least in that respect) only a very small minority of pupils. The heading, 'Other subjects', is to be interpreted widely as a residual category embracing everything else in the curriculum not already covered, except physical education and craft subjects. Subjects included in this chapter may be loosely classified as follows:

Traditional subjects	*'Modern' subjects*	*Interdisciplinary courses*
English	Sociology	Humanities
Modern languages	Government	Integrated studies
Classics	Economics	General studies
Geography	Economic history	Environmental studies
History	Social economics	Social science
Civics	Business studies	
Religious education	Commerce	
Music	Accounting	
Health education		

No single school would offer all of these because of overlapping, since some titles represent distinct methods of presentation rather than complete divergence of content. This permits some compression in considering the common ground, but prevents the uniformity of treatment adopted in Chapter III. There it was possible to analyse a fairly modest number of textbooks and course schemes, either representative or at least typical of the work being done in most schools. This group of subjects does contain basic common-core material, but many schools teach only a minority of the subjects omitting, unfortunately, those syllabuses which contain much of the more interesting statistical material. When such subjects are offered as 'options', they are often not started until the fourth, or even the sixth form. Moreover, the courses provided are less uniform than in the mathematics and science areas and, with notable exceptions, the selection of representative or typical books is correspondingly less reliable as an indication of course content. Thus in all that follows *some* children are being offered the approaches described and of those, again, *some* schools provide them before 16 years, some after, and some not at all.

Geography

Geographers generally are using more and more mathematical techniques, particularly statistical ones. Very gradually these are percolating down to school level. There is a clear need here for more liaison between mathematics and geography teachers so that each subject can enhance the other. The Schools Council project Geography for the Young School Leaver is discussed below as an example of the possibilities available. Other selected instances are contained in the references, by no means an exhaustive catalogue, but one aimed at facilitating the teaching of statistical ideas in geography.

The Geography for the Young School Leaver (GYSL) Project was set up in 1970 with the aim of investigating the special contribution that the geographer can make to the education of 14- to 16-year-old pupils. Special emphasis was placed on the needs of average and below average ability pupils. Three units of pupil material have been published, *Man, Land and Leisure*, *Cities and People* and *People, Place and Work*, together with teacher's guides.[1] The project material has three main objectives: ideas, skills, values and attitudes. Among the skills to be mastered are 'the understanding and interpretation of data' and 'the skill of communication whether it be by written text, diagram, oral discussion or simple cartoon'.

INNER CITY REDEVELOPMENT
(HYDE PARK, SHEFFIELD) CENSUS DATA

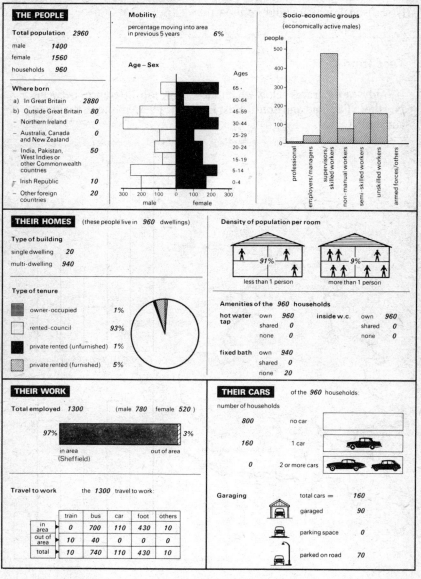

THE PEOPLE

Total population	2960
male	1400
female	1560
households	960

Where born

a) In Great Britain	2880
b) Outside Great Britain	80
– Northern Ireland	0
– Australia, Canada and New Zealand	0
– India, Pakistan, West Indies or other Commonwealth countries	50
– Irish Republic	10
– Other foreign countries	20

Mobility

percentage moving into area in previous 5 years **6%**

Age – Sex

Ages
65 +
60-64
45-59
30-44
25-29
20-24
15-19
5-14
0-4

300 200 100 0 100 200 300
male   female

Socio-economic groups
(economically active males)

people
500
400
300
200
100
0

professional · employers/managers · supervisors/skilled workers · non-manual workers · semi-skilled workers · unskilled workers · armed forces/others

---

THEIR HOMES (these people live in **960** dwellings)

Type of building

single dwelling	20
multi-dwelling	940

Type of tenure

owner-occupied	1%
rented-council	93%
private rented (unfurnished)	1%
private rented (furnished)	5%

Density of population per room

91% — less than 1 person   9% — more than 1 person

Amenities of the 960 households

hot water tap	own	960		inside w.c.	own	960
	shared	0			shared	0
	none	0			none	0
fixed bath	own	940				
	shared	0				
	none	20				

THEIR WORK

Total employed **1300** (male **780** female **520**)

97% ─────────────── 3%
in area (Sheffield)   out of area

Travel to work the **1300** travel to work:

	train	bus	car	foot	others
in area	0	700	110	430	10
out of area	10	40	0	0	0
total	10	740	110	430	10

THEIR CARS of the **960** households:

number of households

800	no car
160	1 car
0	2 or more cars

Garaging

total cars =	160
garaged	90
parking space	0
parked on road	70

Fig. 9 An example of the uses of census data reproduced from the unit, *Cities and People*, Geography for the Young School Leaver Project (Nelson, 1974)

Inherent in the philosophy of the project is the importance of an inter-disciplinary approach. In the teacher's guides there are notes suggesting work in other subject areas including mathematical techniques, particularly statistical, which could be used.

Test Item 4

i) Study the diagrams below which show some job differences between Northern England and South-East England. The map shows the areas concerned.

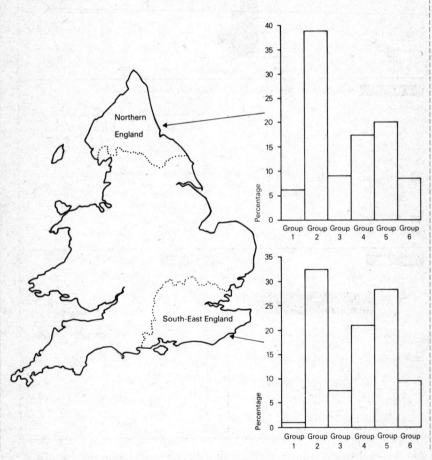

a) Study the diagrams above carefully and then complete the table below.

Types of Jobs by Regions

Group	Percentage of all employees		
	Great Britain	N. England	S.E. England
Group 1 Primary Industries	3·50	6·50	1·50
Group 2 Manufacturing	38·95		
Group 3 Construction, Gas, Electricity, Water	7·64	9·00	7·00
Group 4 Transport, Communications, Shops	18·82	17·50	21·50
Group 5 Professional and Administrative Services	23·02		
Group 6 Other Services	8·07	8·00	9·50
Total	100·00	100·00	100·00

b) What is meant by the term 'primary industries'?

_____

_____

_____

c) Study carefully the table you have completed, then tick those statements which you think are *correct*, and put a cross beside those statements which you think are *incorrect*.

A) The table shows that employment in professional and administrative services in Northern England is above the national average.

B) The Table shows that employment in manufacturing in both Northern and South-east England is below the national average.

C) The table shows that employment in primary industries in Northern England is almost twice the national average.

ii) The LOCATION QUOTIENT for Agriculture, Forestry and Fishing in South-East England is 0·4. Explain:

How this figure is obtained _____

_____

What information this location quotient gives you_____

_____

iii) Study the scatter graph below and then answer the questions.

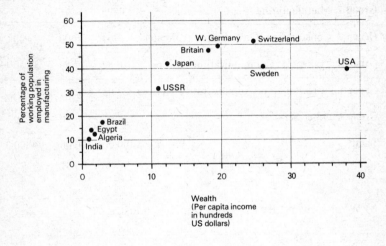

Wealth
(Per capita income
in hundreds
US dollars)

What percentage of the working population of U.S.S.R. works in manufacturing?_____

What is the per capita income of Switzerland? _____

Put a tick beside those statements which you think are *correct*, and put a cross beside those statements which you think are *incorrect*.

A) The U.S.A. is the country with the highest percentage of its working population employed in manufacturing.

B) India is the poorest country.

C) Industrial countries are rich.

D) Poor countries have many manufacturing industries.

E) There is a connection between the wealth of a country and the percentage of its working population employed in manufacturing.

Fig. 10 An example of statistical work reproduced from the unit, *People, Place and Work*, Geography for the Young School Leaver Project (Nelson, 1975)

There is work on the collection and tabulation of data. Questionnaires are used to investigate leisure activities and the need for open space, to discover residents' attitudes, etc. There is little discussion, however, of the difficulties of phrasing questions and getting a representative sample. Census data are incorporated into the work: to show how people travel to work, to measure the importance of a shopping centre, to study changing patterns of leisure and to compare different enumeration districts according to a number of criteria – the types of homes, age distribution, socio-economic groups, etc. Data from five areas are presented statistically in the unit, *Cities and People*, for pupils to compare. One example is reproduced here (Figure 9). It is important for pupils to be made aware of the many uses of census data.

There is much work on the representation of data; statistical diagrams are frequently used for presentation. A few examples are given here to show the scope. Pictograms are employed to show the frequency of ferry services, and car ownership, including prediction (though there is no explanation of the method of prediction or its potential accuracy). Pie charts are used to show the popularity of different types of accommodation for holidays and the pattern of urban/rural land use in different countries. Figures or percentages are often but not always included in the diagrams. Bar charts and histograms occur frequently, occasionally using different colours for extra emphasis. Some charts shown are: an analysis of types of play areas, numbers of tourists and receipts, population densities, age distributions, unemployment patterns and vehicle surveys. The statistical understanding required, however, is not always evident. In a local park survey, the author heard a teacher ask his pupils, 'What information does this histogram give you?', and then comment, 'A difficult question for less able children, many of whom gain satisfaction from a neat diagram but see that as an end in itself.'

Time series are used to compare the number of hours worked and overtime between 1950 and 1970 (though problems over changing definitions are not considered); there is an investigation of the use of a main road at different times and the changing modes of travel over the years are featured.

Scattergrams demonstrate land use at various distances from the city centre. Pupils are encouraged to rank different aspects of a job (security, pay, responsibility, etc.). However, no formal techniques are introduced.

There is an interesting exercise in one unit, where various information is collected to come to a decision. Statistical data are included though there is no formal hypothesis testing. Some of the philosophy of the approach of GYSL is summarized by test item 4, reproduced here (Figure 10). (No source is acknowledged for the data given.) Pupils are asked to read data from the bar chart, and then to do some simple calculations. The second part requires pupils to look at the data carefully and only at the end make a qualitative judgement. This is in marked contrast to the typical mathematical question which requires the calculation of a correlation coefficient or line of regression.

GEOGRAPHY 14–18[2]

This is another Schools Council project incorporating many interesting statistical ideas in its teaching materials, especially in a decision-making context. One example studies the possibility of flooding by considering the correlation between rainfall and discharge from a river. As it is a poor correlation, other facts are brought in to complete the exercise.

History

History is chaps, geography is maps. This crude distinction has some value at school level where much history has been based on facts and events concerning people. Many of the dates involved are still a matter of conjecture, especially the earlier ones. There is scope here for introducing probabilistic models – for example, it is likely, but not certain, that Caesar first came to Britain in 56 BC. Historians, once concerned that pupils should simply remember some basic facts, are now becoming increasingly interested in discussions of validity of events and their timing. Information from periods for which documentary evidence is sparse sometimes rests mainly on archaeological methods, and these can afford useful exercises at school level. The two main ones are: dendrochronology where the pattern of rings on wood reflects local climatic variations from year to year (a close study can establish a continuous tree-ring pattern going back two thousand years or more); and radio-carbon dating which, though less accurate, allows one to go much further back in time and is used mainly in archaeology. This process is subject to error especially with older samples of carbon where decay is so advanced that radiations have become very intermittent and difficult to detect. However, the very presence of error entails a need for statistical treatment. Radioactive potassium has a longer life and, when its use in dating has been properly developed, it can be expected to give dates even further back in the past. These methods yield probability-density functions for events such as the building of Stonehenge; they could fit in with A-level statistics courses.

Statistics was born on the foundations of demographic analysis. Population changes are important for understanding historical development. A population curve over the centuries forms a good basis for discussion. What has been the effect of immigration and emigration? How can we predict population in the future? The age–sex-structure pyramid yields an important historical insight, though care must be taken in interpretation. Social progress can be charted by considering the average weight and height of children at each age over the last century. There is a wealth of such graphical representation in J. S. Maclure's *One Hundred Years of London Education*.[3]

Possible topics for the use of statistical ideas in teaching history (with an obvious overlap with other subjects considered in this chapter) include: poverty, social conditions, equal pay, standards of living, employment levels, transport, social economics, industrial growth, economic and social effects of wars and the depression migration.

HISTORY 13–16[4]

Teaching materials from this Schools Council project include considerable statistical support in the analysis of world population, the development of China and Israel, and industrial and social changes in Britain 1815–51. Bar charts are used to illustrate the growth of consumer goods and industrial output in China in the 1950s, and comparisons can be drawn with a graph of the five-year plan and its revisions, though these could have been made more explicit. In making comparisons between countries, pictograms are used to make fair comparisons of land areas, incomes, and amounts of foreign aid. Those of the population and size of armed forces using large and small men and tanks respectively are confusing (for example, the Chinese is shown nine times the *area* of the Russian to achieve three times his height; the Indian a hundred times the Frenchman, not ten times). The table of population growths and densities against income per head sets the record straight.

The Israeli figures show population growth and proportion of immigrants in separate tables, the comparison being drawn indirectly perhaps because of the danger of confusing numbers of immigrants in the incremental population with that in the total. A bar chart showing Jewish migrations to Palestine and percentage of total residents for an earlier period (1904–56) shows columns of equal widths for periods of 12, 11, 5, 8, 7, and 9 years respectively without leaving spaces to show where the two world wars intervened, for which no data are given. The lack of a consistent scale here also bedevils comparison between column heights to represent rates of migration at different periods.

Some interesting British archive data have been assembled, though care is needed to detect figures which are examples from those which are comprehensive. The freight carryings between Liverpool and Manchester, 1830–33, and comparative costs by various transport modes in 1844, are of the former category, but the mileage of railway route opened 1825–51 and passenger carryings 1838–51 appear to be more generalized. There is a fascinating list published by Chartists showing rotten boroughs returning candidates to Parliament with under 300 and under 200 votes, a distribution of court sentences following the 1830 riots, church attendances by sect at the 1851 census, a chart for calculating rates of poor relief and comparison of total expenditure on this to total population in 1801, 1821 and 1831. Much of this information could fire the imagination of teachers and pupils to produce additional derived statistics, but this does present snags, in that not all the extra desired data are necessarily available and often not all the data given are completely compatible.

Economics

During the last two decades the study of economics has gradually spread from university courses and professional qualifications back to younger students at school. At the same time the economics courses which teachers have attended have become progressively more numerate, while availability of computer facilities has encouraged the insertion of real data into the economic models and so brought a marked increase in the use of statistics.

The composition of many basic texts is well in line with the recommendations of F. Davies[5] on the content of the Middlesex CSE Board scheme. Three of Davies' aims imply statistical understanding and support: that pupils should:

1. Understand the interdependence and interaction of different parts of the economy
2. Acquire the necessary skills to find economic information, evaluate evidence, and suggest solutions
3. Read the media critically.

It could be argued that Davies is here interpreting positive economics to imply that economic theory should be treated along with relative topics in applied economics.

The following important topics occur in the most courses and utilize statistical *method* to compile economic indicators:

Frequency distribution: income distribution before and after tax (whether skewness can be said to be reduced)
Index number theory: retail prices, wages, production, terms of trade, standardization of birth/death rates
Time series analysis: population trends, employment, trade cycle
Other bivariate or multivariate analysis: intersection of employment and inflation (Phillips curve).

Two central areas of study use statistical data as input to accounting procedures:

National income and expenditure accounts, fixed capital formation
Balance of payments.

Many other areas of study draw on statistical data as input to (mathematical) economic models: public finance, banking, money supply, income from capital, wealth, poverty, consumption by commodities, industry by size of firm, employment by industry, incremental productivity of capital and labour, unionization, distribution.

The books themselves fall into several stylistic groups. Representing the traditional standard presentation are revised editions of old-established books, especially those of Cairncross,[6] Hanson,[7] and Paish[8] (originally Benham). These all deal with population, national accounts, balance of payments, banking, and size of firms by using actual data. Many texts include taxation, employment and retail price indices.

The next generation of books moved in several directions. In a desire to make the treatment of theory more rigorous, some writers moved to a more abstract treatment and (implicitly or explicitly) left the user to introduce statistical material for himself, from official sources or from a handbook of applied economics. The texts by Harvey,[9] and Stonier and Hague[10] and, more recently, Barnes[11] and Fleming,[12] are of this kind. Other writers took the opposite view: that the applied material should be made more central, as did Nobbs in his book outlined below.[13] Some have attempted to combine clear theory with factual (statistical) examples, by covering a more modest field (see Stanlake[14]), or by being thorough in only a selected field. Livesey,[15] for instance, uses more real data than many other writers. He incorporates actual examples of observed elasticities of demand for butter compared with margarine into his analysis of consumer behaviour, which extends to a preference survey of brands of goods by earnings, and to turnover by type of shop and by trade. His account of theory of the firm is enriched by similar detail: frequency distributions of company size and of mergers by share value, of industries by percentages of the labour force, analysed in its turn by membership proportions of major trade unions. In macro-economics, regional policy is illuminated by relative unemployment levels in assisted areas and the proportion of new jobs entailing movement of employee from one region to another. Yet in other topics, such as the national accounts and banking, where most authors draw on official figures, Livesey confines himself to theory. Brooman's *Macroeconomics* [16] provides thorough statistical support in this area, and a statistically well-grounded theory course could be devised using these two books in conjunction.

Nevin,[17] G. J. Edwards,[18] and Lipsey[19] have all moved part of the way from the tradition of Benham towards the theoreticism of Stonier and Hague. At the same time, each of these makes particularly good use of some of the examples they give.

Nearly all authors quote figures of the national accounts and employment, and a fair proportion do so for population, public sector, taxation, and banking. The only statistical computation described in enough detail for pupils to master is that of index numbers, which most texts describe, though not all thoroughly enough. This leaves ample scope for books describing the availability, sources, and applications of data, but many of these are mainly descriptive (Lewes,[20] B. Edwards,[21] Edey, *et al.*[22]), very old (Allen,[23] Devons[24]), or sometimes both. As exemplifying the power and usefulness of applied statistics, the most interesting books are the problem-oriented – for example, *The Use of Economic Statistics* by C. A. Blyth[25] (though published many years ago). Blyth considered a number of themes, topics, or problems, discussed the investigation of these from secondary data and, frequently, the compilation of derived statistics using ratios between data from more than one source. Having worked through several of his dozen case-studies (the term was not much used at the time) most pupils should have acquired a good idea how to set about solving other comparable problems. Though a student today would need to use more recent data, the methodology remains sound. An appendix is provided to aid this updating. His examples include:

Decline of the cotton industry, 1947–58
Slump in vehicle production 1956–57
Evaluation of changes in prices and incomes
Attribution of saving and investment
International comparisons of income and output (the detailed difficulties have altered radically with UN accounting methods, but the fundamental problems remain)
Seasonal analysis of fruit and vegetable prices
Import dependency

Nobbs' book, *Economic Problems of the 1970s*, is designed for school use, presumably as an adjunct to his own textbook, *Economics for the Advanced Level*, but it could equally well be used with many others. He gives nineteen case-studies, with varying amounts of background information; some are very detailed statistically, others perceptibly less so. Though he is not the only person to use topic-oriented discussion, he carries this further than the authors of any of the other texts the project looked at. His presentation could be used as a basis for economic team games with far less additional preparation than Blyth's examples would require, apart from being more recent. The background is particularly thin on Giro, metrication, and decimalization, but elsewhere great resourcefulness has been shown in culling press data (from the *Financial Times* and *Sunday Times*) and other less conventional sources. Some examples with associated topics follow:

Concorde evaluation
Number of computers in use (Industry NEDC)
Colour TV growth
Brain drain
Working population and equal pay

Redundancy (Department of Employment)
Unionization (Royal Commission)
Industrial reorganization
Corporation effectiveness (corporation annual reports)
Mergers
Unit trusts (trade association, Whitaker's *Almanack*)
Regional planning, employment levels, and population densities
North Sea Gas forecast reserves and yields
Advertising expenditure
Resale Price Maintenance and effect on distribution: how far did abolition favour supermarkets at the expense of small shopkeepers? (*Self-Service and Supermarket Directory*, *Group Grocer*, Registrar of Restrictive Trading Agreements, *The Economist*).

The approaches to economics teaching exemplified in these books may not be universally, or even widely, used. However, interest may well be generated, especially where interdisciplinary schemes of work are being contemplated.

Other subjects

ENGLISH

As a subject this involves using words as words and is not primarily concerned with numeric or quantified aspects. It is possible (as is done in teaching materials issued by this project team) to use statistical analysis of literary style as evidence of authorship but, in school, discussion of style is mainly qualitative. Over recent decades English teaching has, if anything, moved away from formal analysis in favour of fluent reading and composition. While material used to acquire linguistic skills can benefit from relevance to other parts of the curriculum, statistical matter is not a strong candidate for this as it aims to achieve clarity of expression through tables, curves and diagrams that minimize verbal content in the communication.

MODERN LANGUAGES

Studies of the civilization and culture of France, Spain, Germany, Russia, etc., are now widely thought of as a necessary and motivating adjunct to learning the language and reading the literature of the country in question. Some less able pupils may opt for the cultural studies only.

The content of these courses varies with the individual teacher and the time allotted. Where the language texts include background material over and above that imparted through the language-learning matter, it is mostly not very detailed and dates quickly. Educational newspapers and the like are of more value than ordinary textbooks in this field where topicality and motivation are important. These may at times contain quantified demographic information, industrial and social statistics. Data on different consumer habits in Europe have figured in some television programmes which could be used in the context of these courses.

'Civilization' courses on other countries contain similar topics to those in more detailed studies of Britain in geography, history and current affairs. Though not specific to the particular countries, the sections above on history and geography give a fair idea of the scope of such courses. Particularly well-informed teachers may transcend the limitations of published texts by making specific statistical comparisons between Britain and the foreign country, and by drawing on personal resources and contacts.

CLASSICS

Latin and Greek are now taken by quite small minorities of pupils, and many schools offer no facilities whatever in these subjects. Trends over the last twenty-five years have been towards greater fluency in reading texts *quickly* rather than the meticulous attention to syntax and sentence composition once in favour. The study of Roman or Greek civilization has always been included but, except for military history and a few major building projects, the documentary basis for detailed statistical treatment is lacking. Archaeological dating was discussed above under history. There is scope for an inclusion of this in classical studies.

CIVICS

This subject was often used as a 'filler', timetabled for one or two periods per week, and consisted mainly of constitutional law and citizenship. Its popularity has dwindled in favour of studies in government and social sciences that take into account the number of people or volume of expenditure affected by actual and proposed changes. The switch to these more broadly based ideas may be welcomed quite apart from any use and interpretation of data in their evaluation.

RELIGIOUS AND MORAL EDUCATION

Though listed as a traditional subject, this may or may not be taught in a traditional way – that is as studies of, or stories from, the scriptures and biographic projects of famous and distinguished citizens who exemplified some form of moral leadership. Scholars have, of course, subjected the scriptures to statistical word analysis, on similar principles to those mentioned under English above in seeking to establish authorship and date of the original. Some teachers refer to and discuss these problems, but it is not common practice to perform such tests in the classroom even on a sampling basis (research studies have often involved the complete text). If it were, it is possible that stylistic differences might appear as great between different translations as between different original authors in the same translation. At any event the use of translations, imposed by practical considerations, would inevitably blur the results. Where the discussion is widened to present-day moral community problems, social services, poverty and the like, these do call for support by way of social statistics, the study of how these are obtained locally and nationally, and problems of their interpretation. Rather than following any particular text or type of text, teachers often start with the problems that seem most immediately relevant in their neighbourhood, which might be housing and the homeless, public health, or possibly employment. The pattern varies considerably, as does the time allotted, but the statistical content is likely to be of a kind similar to that of social studies and other interdisciplinary courses, whether it reinforces, complements, or substitutes for these. There are distinct interpretative problems in looking for specifically moral evidence, but statistically this is equivalent to that of singling out any one cause or influence from several that have been combined in the secondary data.

HEALTH EDUCATION

There are good reasons for the use of statistical support in the discussion of the relative importance for health of habits and patterns of conduct. As in other social studies, these topics fall into sharper relief when quantified in empirical terms. Examples where this can be fruitful are:

    Smokeless zones, fuel consumption, and pollution
    Personal smoking
    Research on hours of sleep

Accidents
Alcoholism and drugs
Nutrition studies
Fluoridation and dental health
Transmission of notifiable diseases
Classification of hospital admissions and inmates

MUSIC

This is a subject rather sparingly timetabled considering the widespread interest in it as a leisure pursuit and the opportunities it affords for creative and interpretative talent. Most schools discuss 'Top Twenty' singles charts at one time or another. It is instructive to compile one from preferences expressed in the school and compare it with that published by an enterprising local paper from its own survey of record sales, or with the national surveys. The methodology of these is not well written up, but variations between them are sometimes due to the use of rather small clustered samples of outlets. The chart is an ordinal ranking so in theory the number one in summer may sell only a third as many copies as number one in December, unlike Gold Disc awards.

SOCIOLOGY

The distinction between subjective and objective data leads immediately into deep water in the teaching of sociology. An ethnomethodological sociologist would take the view that all data are so contaminated by the preconceptions of the observer (enumerator) as to provide valid insight into a study of that person's attitudes but not into the phenomena the data are ostensibly portraying. The philosophical implications of this account for the postponement, in most schools, of detailed sociological studies to the sixth form. The substance would centre here on the study of individual behaviour and the explanation of motives in apparently commonplace situations, requiring the observer to detach himself from any part of common culture or background normally taken for granted and to record from an 'ecstatic' (uninvolved) position. It would be a long time before sufficient observations of this kind could be gathered to lend themselves to any statistical treatment, even if the validity of this was not precluded on grounds of definition. In epidemiological or ecological sociology the view is taken that, despite problems of definition and interpretation of events leading to classification errors, some useful indications can be obtained from social statistics if due allowance is made. The use of official and other figures in this way to generalize about social phenomena requires studies of:

a The nature of statistical error in qualitative and, where possible, quantitative terms

b Study of bivariate and multivariate patterns and comparisons of these between distinct points in time

c Tests of significance, especially for differences between two proportions (for example, the proportion of admissions to psychiatric hospital among one-person households against that in a control population).

Where studies are begun at fourth form (or before) they would be likely to demand at least an intuitive treatment of **a** and **b**, such as scattergrams. The inclusion of sociology at this level is not widespread (about 3 per cent of those schools teaching statistics, in the project survey). Its content would be strongly influenced by the interests and enthusiasms of the staff responsible for it. Mode III examinations are relatively more attractive here than in more established school subjects. The statistical support, in schools taking part in our survey, consisted in the main of collecting and presenting primary and secondary data, some sampling theory, forecasting, decision-making, means, and normal distribution – a pattern consistent with taking the subject as far as one reasonably could into epidemiological studies. Only a third of these schools included statistical errors and bias, which might be considered appropriate. However, this was about comparable with the rate of inclusion in most other courses.

GOVERNMENT, POLITICAL INSTITUTIONS

Studies of the legislature rather than of constitutional law can be quantified in some respects, such as levels of representation, electoral data (turnout proportions, swing, etc.), numbers of acts passed and questions asked in Parliament over the years. It is likely that similar information about European procedures and institutions will increasingly be included. The most important statistical skill here is the extraction of comparable data from disparate publications, obtaining and displaying meaningful comparisons. The impact of pressure groups can be studied, using the volume of press coverage over a period compared to the recorded membership (the effect on actual decisions is harder to measure).

The number of courses developed and institutions using them are too few to discern any general trend in statistical content.

ECONOMIC HISTORY AND SOCIAL ECONOMICS

Most courses in economics include elements of these if only as an introductory discussion, recognized to be inadequate, but yielding to an overcrowded curriculum; they also have a natural place in many interdisciplinary curricula. Perhaps many schools would like to devote time to these subjects in their own right, but few in practice find themselves able to do so and they tend to be taken up more fully in higher education social science foundation courses or as one paper in a degree scheme.

Economic history can be subdivided into at least three distinct strands:

a The history of economic thought
b The lives and careers of prominent economists
c The history of economic development – for example, banking and mercantilism, industrialization and demographic implications, technology and growth (for example, numbers employed in industry), and their impact.

Social economics covers comparable ground, though with a distinction in emphasis. The statistical methods needed are chiefly within the realm of time series, bivariate, and multivariate analysis, and as such concentrate on a sector already needed, though often insufficiently studied, in general economics.

BUSINESS STUDIES, COMMERCE AND ACCOUNTING

There is considerable variation in the level to which these are taken as school subjects. At their most sophisticated they can include operational research and decision-making, quality control, stock and production control – all of which demand the use of one or more stochastic models – sales forecasting from time series data with allowance for seasonal variation and trend, and the compilation of separate index numbers for raw material prices, wage costs, and overheads as well as the estimation of profitability in real compared to money terms after segregating the effects of stock appreciation. At the other extreme, some courses go no further than the collection and display of management information (not to belittle the importance of this). The evidence of our own survey would suggest, tentatively, that most courses in this area extend to some treatment of forecasting and decision-making, amounting to at least an appreciation of these but not very often to a study in depth. The use of secondary data is invariably included – this would permit comparisons between the firm and the industry, possibly some assessment of demand changes deriving from changes in population and in real income, and the study of inter-industry effects through input–output tables without going into the theoretical models needed to establish these.

Interdisciplinary courses

It has been argued that insulated subject disciplines occurred in school through looking backwards from specialized ends, not forwards from current experiences. Even so they do relate to one another. Each of the various interdisciplinary schemes mentioned here is intended to cover material from a wide cross-section of subject disciplines as pupils study particular interdisciplinary themes. Nominally distinct schemes thus tend to have much more in common than subject disciplines do, and are here considered together. They have encouraged more widespread use of statistical data than was traditional in the parent disciplines, working towards the use of a statistical approach as part of the thematic link in various subject areas.

The notes that follow refer to individual Schools Council projects rather than to the types of scheme listed on page 57 (the wording is often the same). The projects' thematic orientation generally calls for statistical material acquired or developed locally. The detail the schemes have inspired is too individual and varied to collate and summarize adequately and as yet not fully representative of current methods.

HUMANITIES CURRICULUM PROJECT[26]

The emphasis here is on group discussion of moral and social issues. The role of evidence is considered as documentary, but not always quantified. Graphs and data are included in some of the packs of material on various themes, such as *People and Work* and *Poverty*.

GENERAL STUDIES[27]

This project built up a resource bank of items ranging from newspaper cuttings and book abstracts to photographs and film references. It includes many statistical tables and diagrams, designed for sixth-form use, but with earlier selective applications.

INTEGRATED STUDIES[28]

This is more a concept than a specific work scheme: in principle it is more far-reaching and all-embracing than the others.

Schools from our survey which recorded work with materials from the above projects use primary and secondary data, sampling and collection methods and presentation, some extending this to prediction and decision procedures using intuitive ideas of significance and inference.

HISTORY, GEOGRAPHY AND SOCIAL SCIENCE[29]

The title here indicates the aim to 'interrelate rather than integrate' the several disciplines, the fruits of whose past research it would be wasteful to ignore. The aim is to be achieved more by changed emphasis in methods on the lines advocated by Fenton: 'Instead of giving explanations of data, give the data to explain.'[30] In the social science sector, this project aims to cultivate an impressive list of intellectual abilities:

1 To find information from a variety of sources in a variety of ways
2 To communicate findings through an appropriate medium
3 To interpret pictures, charts, graphs, maps, etc.
4 To evaluate information
5 To organize information through concepts and generalizations
6 To formulate and test hypotheses and generalizations.

All these have statistical connotations, though the last three are not seen that way in the first instance.

SOCIAL STUDIES 8–13[31]

This project was a forerunner of the above. It mainly dealt with history and geography, with involvement of the sciences and English. The aims included 'inquiry skills', recognition of problems from (raw) data, the formulation of hypotheses and design of questions to test them, selection of data needed to verify them. Again this would constitute a kind of apprenticeship to statistically rigorous testing later. Surveys described include one of workers in a local community, and how their needs are met; a survey by age and sex of television viewing habits; one of 'normal levels' of litter in a before-and-after study of the effectiveness of a clean-up campaign; and one on the impact of motorway construction (M4 in Wiltshire).

ENVIRONMENTAL STUDIES[32]

This and the following project are mainly geographic but include engineering, physics, and local history using primary sources derived from fieldwork rather than secondary sources. This approach through activities leads to the progressive development of attitudes and skills required for the observation, recording, interpretation and communication of scientific, historical and geographical data.

PROJECT ENVIRONMENT[33]

This argues for using the environment to set established topics into better perspective. It aims to give the grounding for a responsible view of world problems as an attitude to life. A teacher's handbook, *Ethics and Environment*, covers topics such as population, food, land use planning, and pollution, in which a balanced assessment demands quantification, but available data has to be appraised critically; it cannot always be taken at its face value.

References and notes

1. Schools Council Geography for the Young School Leaver Project, *Cities and People* (Nelson, 1974); *Man, Land and Leisure* (Nelson, 1974); *People, Place and Work* (Nelson, 1975).
2. Schools Council Geography 14–18 Project, various publications. Materials from this project are published by Macmillan Education, Basingstoke. There are five pupil units: *Transport Networks, Industry, Population, Urban Geography* (1978), and *Water and Rivers* (1980), and a teacher's handbook, *Geography 14–18: a Handbook for School-based Curriculum Development* (1977).

3. J. S. MACLURE, *One Hundred Years of London Education 1870–1970.* Allen Lane, 1970.

4. Materials from the Schools Council History 13–16 Project were published in 1977 by Holmes McDougall, Edinburgh. The pupil's books discussed are *Britain 1815–51* in the series 'Enquiry in Depth' and *The Rise of Communist China* and *Arab–Israeli Conflict* in the series 'Modern World Studies'.

5. F. DAVIES, *Starting Economics.* Hulton Educational, Amersham, 1970. See also N. LEE, *Teaching Economics* (Heinemann Educational Books, 2nd edn, 1975).

6. A. CAIRNCROSS, *Introduction to Economics.* Butterworth, 5th edn, 1973.

7. J. L. HANSON, *A Textbook of Economics.* Macdonald & Evans, 7th edn, 1977.

8. F. W. PAISH and A. J. CULYER, *Benham's Economics: a General Introduction.* Pitman, 9th edn, 1973.

9. J. HARVEY, *Elementary Economics,* Macmillan, 4th edn, 1976; *Intermediate Economics.* Macmillan, 3rd edn, 1975; *Modern Economics: an Introduction for Business and Professional Students.* Macmillan, 3rd edn, 1977.

10. A. W. STONIER and D. C. HAGUE, *A Textbook of Economic Theory.* Longman, 4th edn, 1972.

11. R. J. BARNES, *Economic Analysis: an Introduction.* Butterworth, 1971.

12. M. FLEMING, *Introduction to Economic Analysis.* Allen & Unwin, 1969.

13. J. NOBBS, *Economic Problems of the 1970s.* Pergamon, Oxford, 1971. (See also J. NOBBS, *Economics for the Advanced Level.* McGraw-Hill, Maidenhead, 2nd edn, 1975; *Social Economics.* McGraw-Hill, Maidenhead, 2nd edn, 1975.)

14. G. F. STANLAKE, *Introductory Economics.* Longman, rev. edn, 1976; *Macroeconomics: an Introduction.* Longman, 1974.

15. F. LIVESEY, *Economics.* Polytechnic Publications, Stockport, 1972.

16. F. S. BROOMAN, *Macroeconomics.* Allen & Unwin, 6th edn, 1977.

17. E. T. NEVIN, *Textbook of Economic Analysis.* Macmillan Education, Basingstoke, 4th edn, 1976.

18. G. J. EDWARDS, *The Framework of Economics.* McGraw-Hill, Maidenhead, 3rd edn, 1975.

19. R. G. LIPSEY, *An Introduction to Positive Economics.* Weidenfeld & Nicolson, 4th edn, 1975.

20. F. M. M. LEWES, *Statistics of the British Economy.* Allen & Unwin, 1967.

21. B. EDWARDS, *Sources of Economic and Business Statistics.* Heinemann,

1972; *Sources of Social statistics*. Heinemann, 1974.
22. H. C. EDEY, A. T. PEACOCK and R. COOPER, *National Income and Social Accounting*. Hutchinson, 3rd edn, 1967.
23. R. G. D. ALLEN, *Statistics for Economists*. Hutchinson, rev. edn, 1966. (Only very minor changes were made for the revised edition.)
24. E. DEVONS, *An Introduction to British Economic Statistics*. Cambridge University Press, 1956.
25. C. A. BLYTH, *Use of Economic Statistics*. Allen & Unwin, 1960.
26. The Schools Council Humanities Curriculum Project discussion packs were published by Heinemann Educational Books (1970–73).
27. Materials from the Schools Council General Studies Project (15–19) comprise study units and teaching units on thirteen themes, published by Longman and Penguin Education (1972–80), and available from Longman Resources Unit.
28. Schools Council Integrated Studies Project (11–15). *Exploration Man: an Introduction to Integrated Studies*. Oxford University Press, 1972. (Pupil materials are published on three themes: 1. *Exploration Man*; 2. *Communicating with Others*; and 3. *Living Together* (1972–73). There are teacher's guides for units 2 and 3.)
29. Materials from the Schools Council History, Geography and Social Science 8–13 Project are published under the series title, '*Place, Time and Society' by Collins ESL, Bristol*.
30. E. FENTON, *Teaching the New Social Studies in Secondary Schools: an Inductive Approach*. Holt, Rinehart & Winston, New York, 1966.
31. The report of the project was published as Schools Council Working *Paper 39, Social Studies 8–13* (Evans/Methuen Educational, 1971).
32. The Schools Council Environmental Studies Project (5–13) produced four teacher's handbooks, *Teacher's Guide, Case Studies, Starting from Maps* and *Starting from Rocks*, published by Hart Davis Educational, St Albans (1972).
33. The Schools Council Project Environment (8–18) produced four teacher's handbooks, published by Longman: *Education for the Environment, Learning from Trails* and *The School Outdoor Resource Area* (1974); and *Ethics and Environment* (1975).

V. Probability and statistics in primary-school mathematics

This chapter examines the main influences on present primary-school mathematics in England and Wales, with particular reference to work in probability and statistics; and then looks more specifically at the work being done in schools, as shown by the most frequently used textbooks. This information should be useful for secondary-school teachers in assessing the statistical background they may expect in pupils coming to them from primary school. If such background is missing, they may consider incorporating some of the ideas here into their work with pupils in the early years of secondary school.

Influence for change

There is no doubt that the two main influences for change in primary-school mathematics in recent years have been Miss E. E. Biggs, HMI, and the Nuffield Mathematics Project. In the early 1960s Miss Biggs was commissioned to mobilize forces to help spread and consolidate liberal ideas on the learning of mathematics by primary-school children. Many in-service courses were arranged and the first published outcome was Schools Council Curriculum Bulletin No. 1, *Mathematics in Primary Schools*.[1] The Nuffield project in the mid-1960s was instrumental in setting up many teachers' centres and local discussion groups. Their findings resulted in the Nuffield guides for teachers.

Their influence is confirmed in the survey carried out by the Schools Council project, Primary School Mathematics: Evaluation Studies.[2] One of the questions asked of schools was, 'Were there any texts, books or courses you found useful in constructing the school's scheme of work?' The replies gave four major sources:

%
28 *Mathematics for Schools* (H. Fletcher and A. Howell)[3]
19 *Alpha* and *Beta* (T. R. Goddard and A. W. Grattidge)[4]

17 *Mathematics in Primary Schools* (Schools Council Curriculum Bulletin No. 1)

17 Nuffield guides (Nuffield Mathematics Project)

The Nuffield teacher's guides had a direct influence on Fletcher and Howell, since Harold Fletcher had previously been a research fellow for the Nuffield Mathematics Project. The fourth source, *Alpha* and *Beta*, is two series of textbooks for children and we return to these later.

Although there are differences between the philosophies of Miss Biggs and the Nuffield project, they do have many ideas in common. Not least of these is that children should be actively involved in doing mathematics. This leads to a great deal of measuring, counting and representation of findings. A feature of both is that they lead to much more pictorial representation of data, and it is here that there are the beginnings of some work in statistics.

The material from the School Mathematics Project (7–13) had not been published when the research for the Schools Council Primary School Mathematics: Evaluation Studies Project (1972–75) was being carried out. Since the SMP material was published during the lifetime of the Statistical Education Project, and since SMP is so influential at secondary level, we have included a review of this material also.

'MATHEMATICS IN PRIMARY SCHOOLS'

Mathematics in Primary Schools contains many references to work done by children, with the implication that similar work could, and perhaps should, be done by all children. A feature is the way that the same work can be done at different levels by children of different age and maturity.

For example, some 6-year-olds are described measuring the length of shadows and plotting their results. Some 10-year-olds similarly join the points and make some attempt to extrapolate their curve to predict the shadow length at a later time. A simple idea of average is introduced to 7-year-olds by sharing sweets among four of them – the number of sweets being a multiple of four. Some 10-year-olds compare total weights to find the heaviest group of four children and find out what each would weigh if they all weighed the same. Averages are found practically by using strips of paper, cutting and refitting to give constant height. The use of a working mean is introduced to simplify the finding of averages, although care is taken to ensure that no negative numbers arise.

More specifically statistical tasks mention some 6-year-olds counting the dandelions and plantains on part of a lawn, and representing them one to one with coloured poppet beads. Some 10-year-olds in a similar activity sample weeds within a square foot wire frame and are asked to try to predict the number in the whole lawn. A more sophisticated sampling example by the same age-group is to find the incidence of different creatures in a pond, ensuring that the sample includes the use of sunlit regions, shaded regions, weedy regions and moving water regions. No attempt is made though to make the proportion of the total number of samples match up with, for instance, the ratio of the areas of the regions.

A whole chapter is devoted to graphical representation, and emphasis is placed on the gradual increase of abstraction in representation as the children mature. So a traffic census is represented using toy cars with 5-year-olds, labelled cubes with 7-year-olds and a block graph with older children. Quite rightly there is an emphasis on interpretation: 'It is of the utmost importance that, once a graph has been made, it should then be used for further discoveries'. Reference is made to errors, as in fitting a straight line to the results of length of rubber band plotted against weight suspended, when the possibility of deducing that some mistake has been made is discussed.

There is no reference to probability or mention of examples designed to introduce probabilistic ideas.

NUFFIELD TEACHER'S GUIDES

There are two Nuffield guides particularly relevant to the teaching of probability and statistics in primary schools. They are *Pictorial Represent-ation*[5] and *Probability and Statistics*.[6] Of these the first has been much more influential than the second. For example, Williams and Shuard,[7] in their very full survey of primary mathematics today, have a section on presenting information, covering some of the work from *Pictorial Re-presentation*, but nothing on probability or statistics as such.

Pictorial Representation gives its philosophy as, 'Graphs simplify masses of figures, statements and calculations; they are a storehouse of details which can be explained in words. It is possible also that the graph may allow us to obtain information not in the original data'. There is an emphasis on interpretation: 'The interpretation of graphs and inferences made from them form a vital part of the mathematical and social training of our future citizens.' Again a lot of children's work is reproduced. It is perhaps unfortunate that conclusions tend to be along the lines 'the sample was not representative'. That a sample can be representative of a population is surely something we should try to get over.

Nevertheless there are many interesting ideas put forward for possible pictorial representation. Examples are drawn from history, geography, science, music and social surveys. If followed through, then children should receive a good grounding in the collection of data (but not in random sampling), finding the appropriate simple pictorial representation, and in drawing simple conclusions.

As in *Mathematics in Primary Schools* the emphasis is on starting with concrete representation before graduating to more abstract forms. All representation is considered as one to one, so there is no scale problem on the *y*-axis. The five stages envisaged are: **1** using physical objects – two categories; **2** using physical objects – several categories; **3** using constant-size pictures similar to a pictogram; **4** colouring squares – the block graph; **5** colouring bars – the bar chart. Of course, these stages only apply to the frequency distribution type of presentation. They do not apply, for instance, to the graph of children's heights (*y*-axis) against children's names (*x*-axis) which is used as an example of finding the average height by 'levelling out'.

It is unfortunate that the nature of the data collected is not really considered. Nominal, ordinal, interval and ratio scales are all considered together. This means that problems of class intervals, accuracy of measurement and groupings for heights or weights are largely ignored. Included in the very full list of suggested work for 6- to 7-year-olds are: pets owned (nominal), birth months (interval), packets of crisps sold on particular days of the week (ordinal), and number of children with given heights (ratio scale).

Probability and Statistics has many interesting ideas. In the early pages it looks at some statements that could be made – for example 7 out of 10 children enjoy drinking school milk, Burgocars travel 46 miles to every gallon of petrol – and asks what, if anything, they mean. Some of the questions suggested are quite sophisticated. For example, 'There have been 50 fewer car accidents in Burslem than in Newcastle during the last 5 years, so it is safer to drive in Burslem'. This problem would confound children of a much greater age, and there is not much indication as to how the teacher can develop the children's ability to answer this sort of question. The section on pictorial representation raises many problems that are not mentioned in the other guide. There are references to thinking about how best to collect and arrange data, the use of a census, question-naires, random and non-random samples, and the problem of sample size. It is clear that we are considering a much older pupil, perhaps nearing the 13-year-old.

It suggests that probability ideas be introduced by games. Simple experi-ments using dice and spinners, usually approximately unbiased but occasionally biased deliberately, are given to develop ideas of relative frequency, and tied in with 'expected' results. Some simple games are devised some of which are fair and some are not. Sections on sampling, representation and average are rather skimped, though there is an intro-duction to the reliability of an estimate (done practically), as well as sections on the use of random numbers, the histogram and the mode, median and mean.

The effect on schools

The effect of both Miss Biggs' in-service courses and the Nuffield guides was to make many teachers re-think their approach to primary-school mathematics. A large number of schools started writing their own schemes, many local schemes were developed and many new sets of pupil textbooks were written showing their influence in varying degrees. Without a full-scale survey it is not possible accurately to measure the effect in the particular areas of probability and statistics. In the Primary School Mathematics Project survey quoted earlier schools were asked what textbooks and workcards were used. The results showed that of the classes in the survey:

%
63 used *Alpha* and *Beta* (T. R. Goddard and A. W. Grattidge)
18 used *Mathematics for Schools* (H. Fletcher and A. Howell)
14 used *Making Sure of Maths* (T. F. Watson and T. A. Quinn)[8]
14 used BBC *Maths Workshop* workcards[9]

More than one scheme may be found in any class. A further question found that 49 per cent of the schools used the BBC television programme *Maths Workshop* that was being shown at that time. As a measure of the variety of texts available, a total of fifty-three different textbooks and workcards were found in use.

'ALPHA' AND 'BETA'

The specific comments in this section refer to *Alpha* and *Beta*, but much the same could be said of *Making Sure of Mathematics* which has a similar approach and philosophy. The work on statistics is almost entirely concerned with pictorial representation, and very few pages are given over to this topic. The emphasis is on using data printed in the textbook rather than on the children collecting the data themselves. The instructions are detailed and directed, and it is unlikely that the children will come across here some of the awkward problems raised when they collect statistics themselves. There is no emphasis on drawing inferences from data (as there is in *Mathematics in Primary Schools* and *Pictorial Representation*), and no distinction made between sample and population. There is no work on probability in *Alpha* and *Beta*, and only a very small amount in *Making Sure of Mathematics*.

'MATHEMATICS FOR SCHOOLS'

Considering the close connexion one of the authors had with the Nuffield project, it is perhaps not surprising that this set of textbooks tends to follow the suggestions of *Pictorial Representation* with some of the ideas from *Probability and Statistics* in the later books. In each of the Level II Books 3 to 8, and 10, there is some probability or statistics. The two are considered separately. Most of the points mentioned in the earlier comments on *Pictorial Representation* also apply here. The statistics in Book 3 involves collecting simple data, nominal and ordinal (favourite pet, and shoe size) with the request to, 'Write number sentences about your sample'. Later the children are asked to try to predict their height, weight and shoe size for the next year, and are given a very simple queuing problem to discuss in connexion with a supermarket. Book 5 uses the frequency of occurrence of letters in passages of English, and suggests comparison with a passage in a foreign language, with the Morse code, and position of keys on a typewriter. The median and the arithmetic mean – by levelling – are introduced. Children are asked to explain some given line charts about traffic. Book 8 brings in the pie chart and scatter diagrams, and talks in a simple way about correlation. There is an emphasis throughout (certainly within the teacher's guides) that children collect their own data and try to draw more information out of it at the end. Probability is introduced in Book 4 via dice-throwing and comparison with what the children expect to happen. It is not clear on what basis the children are meant to make their 'expectation'. Nevertheless an early idea of relative frequencies approaching a limit is introduced by asking the children what they would expect if $n = 32, 48, 64, 80$. Not all items are linked with 'equally likely' situations (arrows spin on discs split into different size sectors). It is unfortunate that events which are neither impossible nor certain are called 'random'. It would have been far better to call them 'possible'. 'Random' used in this way is bound to conflict with the same word in random sampling. Books 6, 7 and 10 pursue the experimental approach to probability through dice, cards, cubes, drawing balls from bags, etc., with the examples getting harder. Throwing one dice leads on to throwing two dice. There is some simple estimation, two and then more stage tree diagrams, some examples on a 'fair' game, mutually exclusive events, a simulation of a one-dimensional random walk, and the Pascal triangle.

SCHOOL MATHEMATICS PROJECT 7–13

This mathematics course is intended for pupils in middle schools, and claims to allow easy transfer to another modern mathematics course at any intermediate stage. It consists of six sequential units (sets of workcards) which allow pupils to progress at their own rate, but with scope for working in small groups. At the time of writing only the first four units were available, on developing mathematical skills and concepts. The statistical content is limited to representation and constant multiplier graphs.

The section headed 'graphs' includes drawing and reading bar charts, and collecting information into tables from which bar charts can be drawn. The terminology used is rather unusual. A bar chart is called a 'column graph', a line chart is a 'stick graph' and straight-line (constant multiplier) graphs are called 'line graphs'. More worrying is the discrepancy in terminology between these workcards and the SMP lettered books, which pupils may well be using in later years. (See p. 50.)

Unit 2 contains simple representation in the form of reading and completing bar charts. The scales used on the cards vary (10s, 6s, 3s) but no explanation is given or attention drawn to the scales used, though these can present difficulties to the pupil. Each bar is shown touching the next, despite the use of clearly nominal data. Again this is at variance with the approach used in the lettered books.

The problems of definition are sometimes ignored. One card reads, 'Ask each child in your class how many people there are in the family, including themselves. Write the information in a table.' There is no suggestion as to how the information should be processed (for example, use of tally marks) so that the table can be completed. The teacher's notes state that this could be done by the whole class or in groups, but as a method it lays little foundation for handling data.

A further group of cards in Unit 2 asks pupils to draw a column graph from information given about attendance at a swimming bath. As worded, the questions are likely to cause confusion in a child's mind about the meaning of the word 'attendance'. Unit 3 continues the use of graphs to straight-line graphs, but there is little else in the way of statistical experience in these cards.

It seems a pity that there is very little continuity between the set of workcards and the lettered books. Perhaps the last three units will do something to bridge the gap.

BBC 'IT'S MATHS'

At the time of the Schools Council Primary Mathematics report the main BBC mathematics programme for primary schools was *Maths Workshop*. This included simple introductions to probability and scattergrams. This series has since been withdrawn, and the only one containing any statistics for primary-school-age children is now *It's Maths* designed for 9- to 11-year-olds. In the series of fourteen programmes, the second one deals with graphs, and includes a bar-chart of shoe sizes.

The influence from abroad

The approach to primary-school mathematics in Europe is fundamentally different from that in this country. There is far more emphasis on sets, logic and mathematical structure. This has meant that where probability and statistics are concerned the emphasis has been on the probability rather than the statistics. The influence of Tamas Varga of Hungary is widespread, not only in his own country but also in France and elsewhere.[10,11] His work has influenced work in this country through contact with the group of teachers known as the Z Association. This work includes a large number of highly ingenious games designed to develop an insight into probability. The materials used include dice and coins. but also dice of different shapes, obviously biased dice, dice with different coloured faces, sampling bottles, etc. Roulette wheels, icosahedral dice and random number tables are used to simulate samples from different probability distributions. The emphasis is on relative frequency probability, what may be expected, what is likely to happen, all dressed up in some highly motivating games. There is, however, no reference to statistics of the 'collection of data' type.

Another project that has recently had a small impact on the primary-school situation in this country is that of the I O W O (Institut Ontwikkeling Wiskunde Onderwijs (Institute for the Development of Mathematical Education)) in Holland. Their booklet *Look on Luck*,[12] recording work done by 10- and 11-year-olds again emphasizes probability rather than statistics, but does start to link the two together.

Summary

Taken as a whole there are many ideas on probability and statistics being used in this country's primary schools. The emphasis is more on the statistics – data presentation particularly – rather than the probability. The spread of ideas is nowhere near uniform, reflecting the experimental stage which this work has so far reached. The absence of consensus means that children enter secondary school without a common core of statistical knowledge, and some of them without any statistical experience at all. Hence it cannot be assumed that work which is capable of being done by the primary-school child will have been done by him or her.

References

1. Schools Council, *Mathematics in Primary Schools*, Schools Council Curriculum Bulletin No. 1. HMSO, 1965; 4th edn, 1972.
2. The report of the project, by Murray Ward, was published as Schools Council Working Paper 61, *Mathematics and the 10-year-old*, Evans/Methuen Educational, 1979.
3. H. FLETCHER and A. HOWELL, *Mathematics for Schools*: Level I, Books 1 to 4; Level II, Books 1 to 10. Addison Wesley, 1970.
4. T. R. GODDARD and A. W. GRATTIDGE, *Alpha*, Books 1 to 4; *Beta*, Books 1 to 6. Schofield & Sims, Huddersfield, 1969.
5. Nuffield Mathematics Project, *Pictorial Representation*. Chambers, Edinburgh, 1967.

6. Nuffield Mathematics Project, *Probability and Statistics*. Chambers, Edinburgh, 1969.

7. E. M. WILLIAMS and H. SHUARD, *Primary Mathematics Today*. Longman, 1970.

8. T. F. WATSON and T. A. QUINN, *Making Sure of Mathematics*. Holmes McDougall, Edinburgh, 1969.

9. BBC, *Pupils' Workcards*. Prepared for use with the School Television series, 'Maths Workshop'. BBC Publications, 1972.

10. T. VARGA and M. DUMONT, *Combinatoires, Statistiques et Probabilités de 6 à 14 ans*. OECD, Paris, 1973.

11. A. ENGEL, T. VARGA and W. WALSER, *Zufall oder Strategie?* Ernst Klett Verlag, Stuttgart, 1974.

12. IOWO, *Look on Luck*. IOWO, Utrecht, 1974.

Appendices

Appendix A Project survey: the sample and questionnaire

Choosing the sample

The survey was designed to sample 10 per cent of all schools with pupils in the age-range 11 to 16. For administrative convenience the sample was clustered by using a few local authorities. These local authorities were chosen proportionately to represent eight categories defined by the size of population, whether or not schools were fully comprehensive, and the presence or otherwise of middle schools. A ninth category, independent schools, was also included. Table A1 shows the number of schools replying in each of the nine categories.

Table A1 Analysis of schools replying to the questionnaire

Maintained schools		*LEAs with population*	
		$< 500\,000$	$> 500\,000$
Obviously comprehensive	with middle schools	14	8
	no middle schools	28	31
Not obviously comprehensive	with middle schools	41	63
	no middle schools	47	60
Independent schools		37	

The data for constructing the sample frame were drawn from the *Education Authorities Yearbook 1975*. Only authorities whose schools bore the title 'comprehensive', or which showed other unequivocal evidence of non-selection, were placed in the 'obviously comprehensive' category.

Within each of the eight LEA categories about a third of the authorities were selected at random. Approximately 30 per cent of the schools in these authorities were then randomly selected to give the equivalent of 10 per cent of all schools in each category. The independent schools were a 10 per cent random sample of all independent schools.

One authority had undertaken that its schools should not be plagued with further questionnaires before Easter 1976 since it had recently carried out a large survey itself. To save time another authority from the same category was substituted. All the remaining authorities approached granted permission for the questionnaire to be sent to their schools and we were most grateful to them for their help and consideration.

The local authorities whose schools took part in the survey were: Birmingham, Cleveland, Coventry, Cumbria, Doncaster, Dudley, Essex, Gateshead, Gloucestershire, Guernsey, Haringey, Hertfordshire, Humberside, Isle of Man, Kirklees, Leeds, Manchester, Merton, Mid-Glamorgan, Newham, North Tyneside, Northumberland, North Yorkshire, Oxfordshire, Powys, Redbridge, Rochdale, Salford, Scilly Isles, Sefton, Sheffield, Staffordshire, Suffolk, Tameside, Trafford, Wakefield, Waltham Forest and West Sussex.

The questionnaire

SCHOOLS COUNCIL PROJECT ON STATISTICAL EDUCATION 11–16
QUESTIONNAIRE

Please complete and return as soon as possible to the above project, Department of Probability and Statistics, The University, Sheffield S10 2TN

A. *General*
1. Name of school ....
2. Boys/girls/mixed
3. Age-range of pupils ....
4. Is any statistics taught at all anywhere in the school? YES/NO. If NO, turn to section F.

B. *Examinations*
1. What percentage of 16-year-olds are entered for an examination in statistics at
GCE O level.................................... Name of board ....
CSE .... Name of board .... Mode ....
2. Do statistical ideas come into any GCE or CSE syllabuses taught?

	Board	Exam
(a) In mathematics YES/NO		
(b) In other subjects YES/NO		

C. *Teaching material*
1. What published/professionally produced material do you use in teaching statistics 11–16 (please specify)?

	In mathematics	In other subjects
Textbooks (e.g. SMP A–H)		
Work cards		
Schools Council projects		
Case studies		
Material for experiments (e.g. dice)		
Posters and display material		
Films		
Television		
Other		

2. Do you use any home-made material in the teaching of statistics? If so, what?

D. Course content

1. Which (if any) of the following are introduced in the age-range 11–16?

	In mathematics GCE O level CSE Other	In other subjects (please specify)
Published statistics Case studies Collecting data Sampling Randomness		
Bias Sorting and tabulating data Pictograms Pie chart Histograms		
Cumulative frequency Median Mean Quartiles Standard deviation		
Experimental probability Theoretical probability Conditional probability Independence of events Simple inference		
Significance Prediction from figures Making decisions from statistics Indices (e.g. cost of living) Binomial distribution Normal distribution		

2. Are any other important statistical ideas taught?   YES/NO
   If so, what and to which pupils?

E. *Teachers and pupils*

1. How many members of staff are involved in the teaching of statistics?
   (a) In mathematics department .... (b) In other subject departments ....
2. How many of these staff studied their statistics:

	Mathematics department	Other departments
(a) on their own		
(b) as part of a college course		
(c) as part of a degree course		
(d) on local in-service courses		
(e) on national in-service courses		

3. Is the shortage of teachers able to teach statistics felt at your school? YES/NO
4. How far would provision of the following be of use in your statistics teaching (0 = little or no use; 1 = of some use; 2 = very useful)

Mathematics departments				Other departments		
0	1	2		0	1	2
			new textbooks			
			pamphlets on topics (e.g. inference)			
			pamphlets on subjects (e.g. statistics in history)			
			case studies			
			reference source book for teachers			
			theoretical material for teachers			
			work cards for experiments			
			films			
			videotapes			
			tape/slides			
			local in-service courses			
			national in-service courses			

5. What other help would you particularly welcome?
6. Do you feel that the statistical needs of the majority of your pupils are adequately met by the age of 16?   YES/NO
   If NO, please state what you consider to be the major omissions.

F. General

1. Have you any other comments you would like to make on the teaching of statistics in schools?
2. The present project is for children in the age-range 11–16. Do you think it would be worthwhile investigating problems in the teaching of statistics to 16+ pupils?   YES/NO
3. Would you like to be sent:
   (a) a report on the results of this questionnaire   YES/NO
   (b) newsletters from the project   YES/NO

Appendix B Statistics books in common use

In this appendix we consider a number of statistics texts mentioned as being in use in the schools covered by the survey. Some are used as back-up material for the statistics content in mathematics or other lessons; the remainder are more likely to be used in courses for CSE or GCE O-level statistics examinations.

1 School Statistics Panel, *Statistics and Probability; an Introductory Course* (including answers) (Foulsham, Slough, 1969).
   Correlation and Regression, as related to statistics (including answers) (Foulsham, 1970).

Both books are written by Scottish teachers to provide an elementary introduction designed for GCE O-level statistics. They are solid books liberally endowed with examples (and answers). The work is suitable mainly for above average pupils, though the earlier exercises could provide useful practice for other classes.

The first half of *Statistics and Probability* deals with frequency distributions, averages, ogives, dispersion including the standard deviation. The techniques are quite well explained: for example, the use of an assumed mean is introduced through carefully chosen examples. There are many diagrams and the data presented are fairly recent.

The second part neatly relates probability to the binomial and normal distribution, culminating with hypothesis testing including null and alternative hypotheses. A well-constructed example illustrates all the fundamental properties of the normal distribution. (Correlation is treated in the other booklet.)

The text is quite sophisticated and only the most able pupils would be able to use it for individual study. Moreover, it presents a rather one-sided view of statistics. There is a short chapter on abuses of statistics and data collection but this seems to be written almost as a side issue, especially compared to the business of learning techniques. Yet the whole purpose of learning techniques is to use them to analyse data. The context in which the data arise is hardly considered.

The booklet on correlation begins by examining bivariate distributions and the concept of correlation. Various formulae and short-cuts for calculating the product-moment coefficient of correlation are given. Only Spearman's coefficient of rank correlation is considered and no justification for the formula is given. Regression is approached intuitively and then by a curious method involving deviations. Finally, the method of least squares is discussed by a simplified example and a proof of the formula using partial derivatives is given.

This booklet is clearly more suitable for the older, more able pupil. It has a fair number of examples, with answers. There is no discussion of the applicability of correlation or which coefficient should be used in a particular case. However, the basic techniques are well illustrated and presented attractively.

2. K. Lewis and H. Ward, *Starting Statistics* (Longman, 1969).
  E. L. Hanson and G. A. Brown, *Starting Statistics* (Hulton Educational, Amersham, 1969).

These two books adopt, to varying degrees, an experimental approach. Both use CSE questions and are intended as introductory books. They are attractively illustrated and set out; Hanson and Brown use colour to advantage.

Lewis and Ward begin with the collection and display of data. The usual methods of representation (pie charts, etc.) are given, but no comparison is suggested. In the section on averages, the assumed zero method is mentioned, though this is not used for calculating the standard deviation; later on, weighted and moving averages are tackled but few real-life examples are given. Frequency and cumulative frequency curves as well as percentiles are discussed; continuous and discrete data are distinguished later in the book. Sampling and surveys are also discussed. The section on probability is quite short; combinations are approached by listing possibilities but there is no mention of tree diagrams or the laws of probability.

Quite a lot of activities are suggested, but it is a pity that there is little attempt to look at real data as in published tables.

The book by Hanson and Brown covers a much wider syllabus, though many of the topics are presented rather hurriedly. One has the feeling that the authors collected together almost all the topics taught in CSE papers (see Chapter II) and wanted to write a book to cover them in less than a hundred pages. They managed this but the sacrifice of potential explanatory material may be thought a high price to pay.

Collection of data, averages, measures of dispersion (including the standard deviation), the normal distribution, moving averages and weighted averages are covered in the space of thirty-nine pages, within which the authors have commendably included examples of applications of these techniques in everyday life. This pressure on space has resulted in some weaknesses. For example, a block diagram is called a histogram, while no mention is made of how to draw a histogram for data grouped in unequal intervals.

Probability is introduced with some real-life examples and experiments before moving on to the theory and laws of probability. Reasons are given for when to multiply or add probabilities, but are capable of misinterpretation. The binomial distribution is approached via $(F + S)^4$ etc., with a fleeting reference to Pascal's triangle. Two short pages introduce the normal distribution as the limit of the binomial. Four more pages explain the normal probability table and hypothesis testing. Other topics introduced include tree diagrams, sampling, regression, correlation (no formula) and Spearman's rank correlation.

This is not really an introductory book – it includes concepts usually on GCE A-level syllabuses – nor does it suggest a coherent teaching strategy, but it could be used for revision purposes.

3 R. Loveday, *First Course in Statistics* (Cambridge University Press, 1966).
Second Course in Statistics (Cambridge University Press, 1969).

This course was written nearly twenty years ago for the grammar and independent school market and the only substantial revision has been metrication. The data are rather anachronistic and its nature seems unlikely to appeal to the average pupil in a comprehensive school.

The first book is introductory, dealing with the following: frequency and cumulative frequency distributions, measures of location and spread (including grouped data and standard deviation), regression, product-moment as well as Kendall's and Spearman's rank correlation, moving and weighted averages. The final chapter of miscellaneous topics refers fleetingly to some of the more important statistical concepts – sampling and bias, questionnaires and representation of data.

The second book is intended to be the bridge to a rigorous university course. Again it deals with techniques: normal, binomial and Poisson distributions, significance tests (including χ^2) and quality control, correlation and analysis of variance. Loveday states that his central idea is probability but there is no reference to expectation. The book concentrates on teaching pupils how to perform various calculations rather than on fostering an understanding of statistics. For example, though it is used implicitly in the chapter on significance, the central limit theorem is only mentioned at the end of the book.

As a statistical course for pupils these books are not likely to make the pupil aware of statistics as a subject intimately concerned with data.

4 S. Ennis, *Transport Statistics* (Clearway, Birmingham, 1970).
Statistics of Food (Clearway, 1971).
Statistics of Trade (Clearway, 1971).
Social Statistics of Great Britain (Clearway, 4th rev. edn. 1980).

These books contain many facts and figures in the form of statistical tables, diagrams and graphs. The first book gives transport statistics from many different countries. The other three books are mainly concerned with Britain.

The bulk of the books consists of statistical data. Each section contains a few simple questions, asking pupils to read tables or graphs. In the earlier books poor lay-out makes this more difficult, but *Social Statistics of G.B.* is well presented. There are also practical assignments for pupils to manipulate or compare figures, and also to represent them in statistical diagrams. These are rather limited in scope but can easily be extended by the teacher.

One drawback is that the figures date rapidly. It would be helpful to have a short teachers' section showing where each set of figures could be found for up-dating: such a project would be suitable for older pupils. It is a pity that consistent units of measurements are not used in each book. Nevertheless these books are a useful supplement for teaching statistics in geography, mathematics and social studies.

5 B. C. Erricker, *Elementary Statistics* (Hodder & Stoughton Education, Dunton Green, 2nd edn 1970).

In his introduction the author states this book is designed to meet the requirements of G C E O-level students of statistics, people with limited mathematical knowledge requiring some understanding of statistics, and teachers wishing to introduce statistics to students with only an elementary knowledge of mathematics. The faint-hearted may get no further than Chapter 2, which deals with accuracy and, for example, gives the maximum error in division as

$$\frac{x_1 + e_1}{x_2 - e_2} = \frac{x_2\left(1 + \dfrac{e_1}{x_1}\right)}{x_2\left(1 - \dfrac{e_2}{x_2}\right)}$$

with the theoretical aspects being dealt with before the practical application.

The book covers most of the topics listed in the O-level syllabuses of the Associated Examining Board, Southern Universities Joint Board and the Welsh Joint Education Committee. The omissions include conditional probability and tree diagrams, while independent events are assumed to be understood. The book includes a section on skewness, mentions different types of distribution, for example, binomial, normal, unimodal, bimodal, U-shaped and J-shaped, and there is a brief introduction to the use of ratio scales and logarithmic paper. It therefore contains most topics normally included in the statistics section of O-level and CSE mathematics courses, plus a great deal more besides. The inclusion of so many topics necessarily results in some being treated in a superficial manner. For example, the median for grouped data is calculated through the use of similar triangles, but no reason is given for the likely need to do this, or the assumptions that underlie such a procedure.

Early chapters on classification, tabulation and pictorial and graphical representation use data from government publications, for example the *Annual Abstracts* and *Economic Trends*. This gives an element of reality to the examples, but the use of figures published by the Ministry of Labour immediately dates the data. The advice to students 'As the lowest figure to be represented is more than 300 tonnes, break the vertical scale ...' is not adopted systematically in the illustrative graphs that follow.

The book is metricated and well supplied with examination questions from a wide range of examining bodies. These provide experience and aid confidence for any prospective candidate, but they do limit the practical approach to data collection and analysis so essential for any student of statistics.

It is written in a style that would allow the able student to work alone, with reinforcement on points of difficulty or practical interest from the teacher. There are clear lists of rules for tabulation, purposes of pictorial representation and graphs, guides to the collection of statistical data and the design of questionnaires, as well as illustrated examples of the standard arithmetical processes involved in elementary statistics. Any statistics teacher would find the book useful, since it provides a basis of knowledge, ideas and exercises on selected statistical topics. As a text for pupils, however, it lacks the sparkle required to show the application of statistics to the real world situation. This the teacher will have to provide.

Appendix C Aids for teachers of statistics

Equipment

Nearly all the manufacturers' catalogues contain items such as boards to which shapes and designs will adhere, which can be used to demonstrate diagrammatic methods. These basically simple ideas can save a lot of time if already available, but they are quite expensive compared with home-made or traditional methods.

Most of the specific statistics material is connected with the teaching of probability. Some of the simpler items such as loaded dice can be made in class if there is time, but professional ones are convenient, durable, and fairly cheap if they can be bought independently of more ambitious packages which may contain other unwanted contents. As a rule the items which raise the price of full kits are sampling boxes and other simulators which, however well made they may be, tend to have limited use. Though based on traditionally abstract forms (coloured beads, etc.), without relevance to real-life situations these devices are, however fascinating to work with, comparing 'random' results with theoretical distributions.

The most widely used and easily obtained probability kits are those marketed by E. J. Arnold, Invicta and Technical Prototypes. It is regrettably not possible to offer a 'Which?' test on the durability and practical convenience of these, but the contents differ in some respects. All three contain dice (Invicta, plain; Arnold, plain and biased; Technical Prototypes, plain biased and twenty-sided), also roulette wheels, and a small sample device (bottles in Arnold and Invicta, and a specially designed box in Technical Prototypes). For binomial distribution simulations, all include devices which are basic modifications of bagatelle design, the Arnold version with twenty-five marbles, the Invicta with a hundred or more, and the Technical Prototypes version (quincunx) using a large population of grains as in an hourglass. Though the principle is the same, the varying degrees of sophistication are reflected in the prices charged. Arnold and Invicta also include playing cards, and Arnold a fruit machine. The full Technical Prototypes kit is considerably more expensive because of the degree of refinement in the quincunx as well as the inclusion of decimal dice and a bivariate surface. However, they offer school and student versions for a lower price range, omitting the roulette wheel and quincunx, but including in all three of the versions rod populations in a distribution which can be used to simulate variability, though in essentially discrete steps. All the kits contain instruction books and most of the components are available separately.

Nearly all educational suppliers offer spinners, distribution demonstrators (by placing counters on spikes, etc.) solid geometry sets from which ten-sided dice could be made in class, and various abacus, wood-block, and rod sets which have some statistical applications. Various number base gadgets are available, including punched cards from Invicta. This firm supply an advertising film *Resources for Mathematics* demonstrating their equipment, though a visit by a representative might be preferable. There is no doubt that many of these items are attractively produced, and possibly more accurately made than is easy to achieve in the classroom; provided budgets permit, they also save time.

A slightly different form of probability kit is produced by Oliver & Boyd. This has ten sealed tubes which contain, in varying numbers and colours, ball bearings dice, coins or cubes. A series of experiment cards is provided, with three experiments suggested for each tube, each providing a win or lose situation, but with different probabilities of success. There are also spare tubes, dice, discs and cubes. Also included are specially prepared sheets for speedy recording of results of up to fifty trials. These give an instant picture of the number of successes at any stage of the experiment, and their use is not limited to the experiments in the kit.

The variety of apparatus that can be designed for statistical experiments is illustrated in *Statistical Teaching Aids* edited by T. Szmidt and A. F. Bissell (Institute of Statisticians, 1977).

A selection of simulation games is marketed by Management Games. This firm produces simulation games for various age-groups of students in economics, geography, history, social science, science and mathematics. The mathematics section includes a statistics workshop, which introduces statistical sampling, from a practical viewpoint, for students from 14 years old upwards.

Addresses
E. J. Arnold, Butterley Street, Leeds, LS10 1AX
Invicta Plastics, Oadby, Leicester, LE12 4LB
Management Games, 11 Woburn Street, Ampthill, Bedford, MK45 2HP
Oliver & Boyd, Croythorn House, Ravelston Terrace, Edinburgh, EH4 3TJ
Technical Prototypes, 2 New Park Street, Leicester, LE3 5NH

Audio-visual resources

TELEVISION FOR SCHOOLS

We consider here television series which are expected to continue running into the foreseeable future; those in their final year or two of showing; and those no longer broadcast but which are available for sale or hire to educational institutions.

The first category gives schools a chance to preview before deciding whether to use them in subsequent years, though Independent Television show previews of new programmes before each school term.

The second category programmes clearly require recording if they are needed for future years. The BBC copyright concessions on recording 'off-air' BBC school and further education broadcasts sponsored by the Schools Broadcasting Council allows such recordings, subject to certain conditions, one of which is that the recordings are destroyed within three years of their being made. ITV educational programmes can be recorded if a licence to record has been granted to the local education authority.

BBC maths series with some statistical content include:

'It's Maths' (9–11 years). Programme 2, *Graphs* (includes bar-chart of shoe sizes). Last planned showing 1980–81.

'Everyday Maths' (14–16 years, low ability). Programmes 9 and 10, *Say it With Figures*, Parts 1 and 2 (questionnaires, interviewing, presentation of data, sampling). Last planned showing 1981–82.

'Maths Topics' (13–16 years) for GCE/CSE (grade 3 and above). Programme 6, *Data Collection* (including the census of population and sampling); Programme 7, *Data Representation* (diagrammatic presentation); Programme 8 *Data Reduction* (measures of central tendency and measures of spread); Programme 9, *Probability* I (including relative frequencies); Programme 10, *Probability* II (equally likely outcomes and the probability scale). This series is designed to be recorded, and used as part of a library of resource material.

The emphasis in the programmes transmitted by the ITV companies is less on statistical (or mathematical) theory, and more on fields of application:

The middle school series 'Look Around' (environmental science) uses data and measurement in some of its programmes. These include: 1. *Energy*; 3. *Water Resources*; 4. *Food*; 6. *Air – Smoke and Pollution*; 7. *Transport*; 8. *Refuse, Salvage and Recycling*; 9. *Noise Control*; 10. *Population*, including demographic problems and trends.

The 'Facts for Life' series (for 15 +) relate health topics to anatomy and physiology, but some of them use statistical evidence: 1. *Drug dependency* (drink and smoking); 5. *Contraception and VD*; 6. *Diet and exercise* (health of heart and lungs).

The 'It's More Life' biology series (13–16 years) has a programme (No. 7) entitled, *How to Weigh an Island*.

Teachers' notes can be obtained for all these programmes, and pupil material for many of them.

Among the previous BBC programmes now available for purchase is the 'Mathematics in Action' series on statistics. This is a series of ten programmes designed for post-O-level students, and includes programmes on statistical inference, the binomial and normal distributions, sampling and correlation. Also available is Series 2 of the 'Middle School Mathematics' programmes, again entitled *Statistics*. There are six programmes covering frequency distribution, averages and spread, sampling, chance and correlation. Each programme runs for twenty minutes and is available from BBC Enterprise Film Sales. Film of some ITV schools programmes can be obtained from the Granada Television Film Library.

OTHER TELEVISION PROGRAMMES

Past BBC programmes from some series using applied statistics are available on film. Among the more useful series. 'Economics of the Real World' offers for hire nearly half of its programmes including: *The Budget* (3); *Inflation* (6); *Balance of Payments* (7); *Getting Richer* (8); *Pollution* (10); *The Price of Labour* (15). Many back numbers of *Horizon* are available; these are rather longer, often between forty and fifty minutes. Two medical programmes which consider statistical evidence are: *Cancer – the Smoker's Gamble* and *A Disease of Our Time – Heart Attacks* (the latter for hire, the former for sale only). From the 'Profit by Control' series programmes 2 and 7 on sales forecasting and stock control, each running twenty-five minutes, draw on statistical background.

Programmes made for the Open University include those for MDT241 'Statistics: an Interdisciplinary Approach', of which *Questions for the Statistician* and *Take a Sample* could be relevant in many situations, while the T100 course has a programme entitled 'Statistics and Reliability', in the industrial context. Other possibilities include selected programmes from the Open University courses mentioned in the section on in-service courses (page 121).

Other resources

Since the survey was carried out a new journal *Teaching Statistics* has been launched. It is sponsored by the Applied Probability Trust, the Institute of Statisticians, the International Statistical Institute and the Royal Statistical Society, and is published three times a year. The journal seeks to help teachers of geography, biology, the sciences, social science, economics, etc., to see how statistical ideas can illuminate their work and to make proper use of statistics in their teaching. It also seeks to help those who are teaching statistics and mathematics with statistics courses. The emphasis of the articles is on teaching and the classroom. The aim is to inform, entertain, encourage and enlighten all who use statistics in their teaching or who teach statistics. (Subscription details can be obtained from the Editorial Office, Department of Probability and Statistics, University of Sheffield, Sheffield S10 2TN.)

The Educational Foundation for Audio Visual Aids publish two catalogues: 1 with the Association for Liberal Education, *Films for General Studies*, which consists mainly of (reviewed) feature films but includes two films on Consumer Association car tests which use some applied statistics; and 2 a classified guide to sources of educational film material. This is an indispensable reference work for anyone making use of film in schools. It lists nearly four hundred distributors of films, loops, strips, etc., with a list of subject areas covered in the collection of each and cross-indexed by subject and by projection equipment. Thus if you have a particular type of projector you can immediately look up all distributors in the list who can supply material you could use. The larger collections like Rank and many of the industrial public relations libraries such as those of Unilever, British Steel, British Transport, and Ford Motors, and the petroleum companies, do have selections that include some quantified information with background material to set it in context. Indeed, even when the data are weak, it is often possible to use these films as background and then supplement them, provided the notes are good enough to indicate which data to look up. One omission from the list is Millbank

Films, whose film, *One Million Hours*, concerning industrial accidents could be used in just this sort of way, especially for impending school leavers. Another example is the cartoon based on Darrell Huff's book, *How to Lie with Statistics* (Penguin Books, 1973), distributed by Video Arts. Two organizations which supply newsletters to keep you up to date, as well as more permanent material, are the British Film Institute and the British Universities Films Council.

On industrial statistics several useful series on production control, quality control, stock control, and activity sampling are available (to buy) from the British Productivity Council or (to hire) from the Central Film Library. These are supplied only in 16 mm sound versions. Szmidt's *Statistical Teaching Aids* (Institute of Statisticians, 1972) mentions several others in this field, mainly of American origin.

Quite a long series of topics is available on tape-slide from Prismatron entitled 'Statistics Computing and Operational Research'. Though related, the individual topics are self-contained. Of the first fifteen topics issued in the statistics section, seven are for students without prior knowledge and could be acceptable for the under 16-year-olds. These include: *Statistical Diagrams*; *What is 'Average'?*; *Sampling and Questionnaires*; *Probability* I and II; *Decision Theory*; *Time Series Analysis*. (There are now thirty-one tape-slide sequences in this series.) These are followed up by a series on distributions of which the first may be fairly intuitive, but the others soon lead to deeper water. An inspection copy service is available. It seems likely that teachers might wish to use the visual material more slowly and adapt the tape commentary accordingly.

BBC Enterprises also supply 8 mm film loops related to some of their programmes, which can be used for recall, in place of unavoidably missed episodes, or after the original series has been superseded. The filmstrips intended for radio-vision are more properly considered as ancillary to the radio series. Missed radio programmes are covered by an emergency tape service, from Theatre Projects Services.

Useful addresses

BBC Enterprises (film hire), Woodstow House, Oundle Road, Peterborough, PE2 9PZ; (film sales), Villiers House, The Broadway, London, W5 2PA

BBC Publications, 35 Marylebone High Street, London W1M 4AA

British Film Institute, 127 Charing Cross Road, London WC2

British Universities Films Council, Royalty House, 81 Dean Street, London W1V 5HB

Central Film Library, Government Building, Bromyard Avenue, London W3

Educational Foundation for Audio-Visual Aids, Paxton Place, Gypsy Road, London SE27

Granada Television Film Library Ltd, Manchester 3

Millbank Films Ltd, Thames House North, Millbank, London SW1P 4QG

Prismatron Productions Ltd, 9 Gloucester Crescent, London NW1 7DS

Theatre Projects Services, Ltd, 11–13, Neals Yard, London WC2 9DP

Video Arts Ltd, 68 Oxford Street, London W1V 3FA.

In-service and other courses for statistics teaching

In this section are described some of the opportunities available for teachers to improve their knowledge of statistics and its applications. It includes only nationally available courses which may be undertaken by teachers either in addition to their normal work or on secondment. Most of these courses are run by the Department of Education and Science or with its approval, as part of their in-service training programme, and the Open University, as part of their degree courses. Many courses will have fleeting reference to statistics; those mentioned here include some specific statistical content.

COURSES IN DES HANDBOOKS

The DES organize short and long courses for teachers and others engaged in the educational service in England and Wales. Details of these are given in two books available from the DES (HFEI, Elizabeth House, 39 York Road, London SE1 7PH): *Programme of Long Courses* and *Programme of Short Courses*. The references used here are those designated by the handbooks. The following details are from the course lists for 1979/80, but many similar courses will be run in subsequent years.

The mathematics courses will probably contain some reference to statistics. There is only one short course in the 1979/80 list which deals specifically with statistics: N481 'Statistics in Comprehensive Schools'. N481 is intended for teachers of mathematics in secondary schools. This ten-day course will help teachers of older pupils in secondary schools, especially at the sixth-form level and those concerned with A-level teaching, to acquire a foundation upon which to place an intelligent treatment of the subject at all levels.

T168a, 'Statistics through its Uses', is a long course of one term's duration and is aimed at teachers in user subjects (not mathematics teachers).

A number of universities (such as Keele and Nottingham) run courses leading to an MSc in mathematical education, with statistics as an option. There are also a number of BEd and Diploma courses concerned with the teaching of mathematics. All these courses involve one year of advanced study, leading to a certificate.

There are one-year full-time courses for those with little background in mathematics who wish to find out more about modern developments. Similar one-term full-time courses are also available. Some courses mention statistics in particular but all the courses make a general reference to recent mathematical innovations and this may well include statistics. Finally, there are a number of part-time courses. In particular the Polytechnic of Wales offers a post-graduate diploma in statistics (CNAA) as a two-year part-time course. This is designed to give an in-depth study of statistics, both theoretical and practical.

THE OPEN UNIVERSITY

The Open University was inaugurated on 23 July 1969. It tries to interpret the word 'open' as broadly as it can. It chooses its students solely on the grounds of the facilities it can provide and demands no formal entry qualifications. The Open University places as few restrictions as possible on the choice of courses a student may take. It has pioneered many new types of course according to spheres of interest rather than being bound by narrow subject classifications. Thus many of the courses are interdisciplinary.

For reference purposes the following code letters are used: D = Social sciences, E = education, M = mathematics, S = science, T = technology. There are three levels of course, coded by the most significant digit: 1 = foundation, 2 = second level, 3 = third level.

Most full credit courses consist of thirty-two ten-hour teaching units, while half credits (asterisked below) have sixteen units. They are all correspondence courses though each one is backed up by a series of television and radio broadcasts. Assignments for each course are marked by a course tutor who holds occasional tutorials for students. Some courses are available only as part of an undergraduate programme, but others are available as single subjects. Courses are sometimes rewritten or replaced, but original versions of the course material may be available from libraries and booksellers.

There are a number of courses which involve statistics and its applications:

M101, 'Mathematics: a Foundation Course'. This introductory course has three units on some of the basic concepts of probability and statistics.

M341, 'Fundamentals of Statistical Inference'.* This course develops statistics in a mathematically rigorous way justifying results often quoted but seldom proved, and the application of statistics in estimation and hypotheses testing.

MDT241, 'Statistics: an Interdisciplinary Approach'.* This course shows the wide scope of statistical applications, after considering the basic theory. The central philosophy is that statistics is a single subject and though there may be different specific techniques in different fields, the core of the statistical argument is common to all. No previous mathematical knowledge is assumed.

D101, 'Making Sense of Society'. Statistics is one of the tools used in this foundation course.

D291, 'Statistical Sources'.* This course aims to enable students to acquire the skills necessary to find, use in descriptive ways, and critically interpret published statistics. No previous knowledge is required; the emphasis is on practical ways to find and present relevant information.

D301, 'Historical Data and the Social Sciences'. This includes four weeks' work on the quantative analysis of historical data.

DE304, 'Research Methods in the Social Sciences and Education'. This includes the collection (by questionnaires and sampling), interpretation and evaluation of data.

DS261, 'An Introduction to Psychology'.* Emphasis is laid on the develop-

* A half-credit course.

ment of the elementary skills of experimental design and statistical analysis. (A re-make of this course is planned for 1981.)

S323, 'Ecology'.* This relatively new subject relies heavily on statistical information.

SM351, 'Quantum Theory and Atomic Structure'.* Here the basic ideas of probability and statistics are used to develop the Schrodinger wave equation and the interpretation of the wave function.

T101, 'The Man-made World: a Foundation Course.' In this introductory technology course, the handling of quantitative data is discussed. T101 is a revised version of this course, available from 1980.

T341, 'Systems Modelling'.* This course considers the use of quantitive models and computer methods in the making of major decisions.

The great majority of correspondence texts can be purchased through the OU Marketing Division (P O Box 81 MK7 6AT), or from large booksellers. Some are available on loan from public libraries and institute libraries. This does not hold for the supplementary materials such as assignments and the supporting notes and list of broadcast times for the radio and television programmes, many of which contain material of interest to teachers and, potentially, to older pupils.

Open University addresses include:

For details of course material for sale: Open University Educational Enterprises Ltd, 12 Cofferidge Close, Stony Stratford, Milton Keynes MK1 1BY

For details of undergraduate programmes: The Admission Office, The Open University, P O Box 48, Milton Keynes MK7 6AB

For details of courses for associate students and post experience courses: The Associate Student, Central Office, The Open University, P O Box 76, Milton Keynes MK7 6AN

OTHER OPPORTUNITIES

Other nationally based courses include the correspondence courses available for those wishing to sit for the examinations of the Institute of Statisticians, (36 Churchgate St, Bury St Edmunds IP33 1RE) who also provide a list of colleges teaching their syllabus. London external degrees could suit the more adventurous.

For those requiring a deeper theoretical grounding as well as knowledge of recent advances, there are M Sc courses in probability and statistics. The following universities run such courses which can often be followed part-time; the assessment is usually by dissertation and a written examination: Aberystwyth, Aston, Bath, Belfast, Birmingham, Bradford, Bristol, Brunel, Cambridge, Cardiff, City (London), Dublin, Dundee, Edinburgh, Essex, Exeter, Glasgow, Hull, Kent, Lancaster, Leeds, Liverpool, London (Birkbeck, Imperial, Queen Mary, Royal Holloway and University Colleges), L S E (London School of Economics), London School of Hygiene

* A half-credit course.

and Tropical Medicine, Manchester and UMIST (University of Manchester Institute of Science and Technology), Newcastle-upon-Tyne, Nottingham, Oxford, Reading, St Andrews, Salford, Sheffield, Southampton, Strathclyde, Sussex, Swansea, UWIST (University of Wales Institute of Science and Technology), and Warwick.

A booklet giving general information about these courses may be obtained from the Secretary, Department of Statistics, The University, Newcastle-upon-Tyne NE1 7RU.

There are also local opportunities. A variety of courses are run by university extra-mural departments, polytechnics, colleges of education and technical colleges. Evening classes, run by the Workers' Educational Association or by the local education authority, often include more technical work. Finally, there are courses run by the local mathematics advisers. If there are no courses on statistics in your area and you feel that a course would be valuable, why not ask for one to be put on? Many places would be delighted to oblige as they would be assured of at least one participant in the course!

References for teaching statistics

The appearance of a book or an article in this list does not mean that the project team necessarily agrees with what is written. Similarly, the absence of a book or article does not mean the team disagrees with it – it probably means it was missed in the project's review.

BOOKS

The following list does not include the many sets of modern mathematics textbooks that include statistics. It does not include textbooks at the undergraduate level or above, except in so far as they are of general interest to teachers in schools.

Books for pupils aged 11–16, including textbooks
BIBBY, J. M. *Living Statistics*. Longman, 1972.
CAMPBELL, I. *Statistics*. Longman, 1971.
DAUGHERTY, R. *Data Collection*. Science in Geography, 2. Oxford University Press, 1974.
DAVIS, P. *Data Description and Presentation*. Science in Geography, 3. Oxford University Press, 1974.
ERRICKER, B. C. *Elementary Statistics*. Hodder & Stoughton Educational, Dunton Green, 1970.
FIELKER, D. S. *Statistics*. Topics from Mathematics Series. Cambridge University Press, 1967.
Towards Probability. Topics from Mathematics Series. Cambridge University Press, 1971.

GILES, R. (ed.). *Statistics of Food*. Statistics for Schools Series. Clearway. Birmingham, 1971.

Statistics of Trade. Statistics for Schools Series. Clearway, 1971.

Transport Statistics. Statistics for Schools Series. Clearway, 1969.

HANSON, E. L. and BROWN, G. A. *Starting Statistics*. Hulton Educational, 1969; rev. edn, 1977.

HUFF, D. *How to Lie with Statistics*. Gollancz, 1954; Penguin Books, Harmondsworth, 1973.

IOWO (Institut Ontwikkeling Wiskunde Onderwijs (Institute for the Development of Mathematical Education)). *Look on Luck*. IOWO, Utrecht, 1974.

JOHNSON, D. A. and GLENN, W. H. *The World of Statistics*. John Murray, 1964.

JONES, L. *Statistics*. Macdonald Educational Mathematics Colour Units. Macdonald Educational. 1974.

JOY, R. R. *Statistics*. Macmillan, 1966.

KNOTT, M. J. P. *Statistics and Probability*. 2 vols. Warne, 1969, 1972.

LEWIS, K. and WARD, H. *Starting Statistics*. Longman, 1970.

LOVEDAY, R. *First Course in Statistics*. Cambridge University Press, 1966.

MCCULLAGH, P. *Data Use and Interpretation*. Science in Geography, 4. Oxford University Press, 1974.

MORONEY, M. J. *Facts from Figures*. Penguin Books, Harmondsworth, 1969.

MURDOCH, J. and BARNES, J. A. *Statistics: Problems and Solutions*. Macmillan, 1972.

Nuffield Mathematics Project, *Probability and Statistics*. W. & R. Chambers, Edinburgh/John Murray, 1969.

School Statistics Panel, *Correlation and Regression*. Foulsham, Slough, 1970.

Statistics and Probability: an Introductory Course, Foulsham, Slough, 1969.

Schools Council Mathematics for the Majority Project, *Luck and Judgement*. Hart-Davis Educational, St Albans, 1971.

SHERLOCK, A. J. *Introduction to Probability and Statistics*. Edward Arnold, 1964.

URQUHART, D. M. *Statistics*. Edward Arnold, 1970.

WALKER, J. A. and MCLEAN, M. M. *Ordinary Statistics*. Edward Arnold, 1973.

General books for students aged 16–18, including textbooks

ADLER, I. *Probability and Statistics for Everyman*. Dobson, 1963.

ADLER, H. L. and ROESSLER, E. B. *Introduction to Probability and Statistics*. W. H. Freeman, Reading, 1977.

BACKHOUSE, J. K. *Statistics: an Introduction to Tests of Significance*. Longman, 1967.

BARTHOLOMEW, D. J. and BASSETT, E. E. *Let's Look at Figures*. Penguin Books, Harmondsworth, 1971.

BROOKES, B. C. and DICK, W. F. L. *Introduction to Statistical Method*. Heinemann Educational Books, 1969.

BULMER, H. G. *Principles of Statistics*. Oliver & Boyd, Edinburgh, 1965.

CLARKE, G. M. and COOKE, D. *A Basic Course in Statistics.* Edward Arnold, 1978.

DAVID, F. N. *First Course in Statistics.* Griffin, High Wycombe, 1971.
Games, Gods and Gambling. Griffin, High Wycombe, 1962.

DODES, I. A. *Introduction to Statistical Analysis.* Butterworth, 1977.

DURRAN, J. *Statistics and Probability.* School Mathematics Project. Cambridge University Press, 1970.

EHRENBERG, A. S. C. *Data Reduction: Analysing and Interpreting Statistical Data.* Wiley, New York, 1975.

ERRICKER, B. C. *Advanced General Statistics.* Hodder & Stoughton Educational, Dunton Green, 1971.

FREUND, J. E. *Modern Elementary Statistics.* Prentice-Hall, Englewood Cliffs, 1974.

GREER, A. *A First Course in Statistics.* Stanley Thornes, Cheltenham, 1980.

HABER, A. and RUNYON, R. P. *General Statistics.* Addison-Wesley, 1978.

HARPER, W. M. *Statistics.* Macdonald & Evans, Plymouth, 1977.

HAYSLETT, H. T. *Statistics.* Made Simple Books. W. H. Allen, 1973.

HOEL, P. G. *Elementary Statistics.* John Wiley, New York, 1976.

HUFF, D. *How to Take a Chance.* Penguin Books, Harmondsworth, 1970.

ILERSIC, A. R. *Statistics.* HFL, 14th edn, 1980.

LEONARD, J. M. *Statistics – the Arithmetic of Decision Making.* Hodder & Stoughton Educational, Dunton Green, 1971.

LOCKWOOD, E. H. *Statistics – the How and the Why: an Introduction Course*, John Murray, 1969.

LOVEDAY, R. *Practical Statistics and Probability.* Cambridge University Press, 1974.
Statistical Mathematics, Cambridge University Press, 1973.
Statistics. Cambridge University Press, 1970.

MALPAS, A. J. *Experiments in Statistics.* Oliver & Boyd, Edinburgh, 1969.

MEYER, P. L. *Introductory Probability and Statistical Applications.* Addison-Wesley, 1970.

MULHOLLAND, H. and JONES, C. R. *Fundamentals of Statistics.* Butterworth, 1968.

MURDOCH, J. and BARNES, J. A. *Basic Statistics: Laboratory Instruction Manual.* Macmillan, 1974.

ORMELL, C. P. *An Introduction to Probability and Statistics.* Oliver & Boyd, Edinburgh, 1968.

PEARSON, E. S. and KENDALL, M. G. (eds). *Studies in the History of Statistics and Probability.* Griffin, High Wycombe, 1970.

RATCLIFFE, J. F. *Elements of Mathematical Statistics.* Oxford University Press, 1967

REICHMANN, W. J. *Use and Abuse of Statistics.* Penguin Books, Harmondsworth, 1970.

Schools Council Sixth-form Mathematics Project, *Introductory Probability.* Heinemann Educational Books, 1975.

School Mathematics Project, *Statistics and Probability*. Further Mathematics Series, V. Cambridge University Press, 1971.

Scottish Mathematics Group, *Statistics and Probability*. Modern Mathematics for Schools Series. Blackie, Glasgow, 1972; rev. edn, Chambers, Edinburgh, 1977.

SKIPWORTH, G. E. *Exercises and Worked Examples in Statistics*. Heinemann Educational Books, 1971.

VESSELO, I. R. *How to Read Statistics*. Harrap, 1962.

WALPOLE, R. E. *Introduction to Statistics*. Macmillan, New York, 1974.

WEAVER, W. *Lady Luck: the Theory of Probability*. Heinemann Educational Books, 1964.

Books for teachers

ABBOTT, D. *Advanced Statistics Questions*. Methuen Educational, 1969.

ADAMS, W. J. *The Life and Times of the Central Limit Theorem*. Kaedmon, New York, 1974.

AITCHISON, J. *Choice against Chance: an Introduction to Statistical Decision Theory*. Addison-Wesley, 1970.

ARMORE, S. J. *Elementary Statistics and Decision Making*. Charles E. Merrill, Columbus, 1973.

ASH, R. B. *Real Analysis and Probability*. Academic Press, 1972.

BARNETT, V. *Comparative Statistical Inference*. John Wiley, New York, 1973.
Elements of Sampling Theory. Hodder & Stoughton Educational, Dunton Green, 1975.

BROOKES, B. C. *Notes on the Teaching of Statistics in Schools*. Heinemann Educational Books, 1957.

BURFORD, R. L. *Statistics – a Computer Approach*. Charles E. Merrill, Columbus, 1968.

CROCKER, A. C. *Statistics for the Teacher*. NFER Publishing, Windsor, 1974.

EPPS, P. and DEANS, J. *Mathematical Games*. 2 vols. Macmillan Education, Basingstoke, 1972, 1976.

FEDERER, W. I. *Statistics and Society*. Marcel Dekker, New York, 1973.

FELLER, W. *An Introduction to Probability Theory and its Applications*, Vol. I. John Wiley, New York, 1968.

FREUDENTHAL, H. *Mathematics as an Educational Task*. Chapter 18, 'Probability and statistics'. D. Reidel, Dordrecht, 1973.

FREUND, J. E. *Modern Elementary Statistics*. Prentice-Hall, Englewood Cliffs, 1973.
Statistics – a First Course. Prentice-Hall, Englewood Cliffs, 1976.

HACKING, I. *The Emergence of Probability: Philosophical Study of Early Ideas about Probability, Induction and Statistical Inference*. Cambridge University Press, 1975.

HASTINGS, N. A. J. and PEACOCK, J. B. *Statistical Distributions*. Butterworth, 1974.

HOPE, C. and BEAUMONT, G. *The Teaching of Statistics.* Association of Teachers of Mathematics, Nelson, Lancs, 1964.

Incorporated Association of Assistant Masters, *The Teaching of Mathematics.* Chapter IX, 'Teaching of statistics'. Cambridge University Press, 1957.

KENDALL, M. G. and BUCKLAND, W. R. *A Dictionary of Statistical Terms.* Longman for ISI, 1975.

KENDALL, M. G. and PLACKETT, R. L. (eds). *Studies in the History of Statistics and Probability.* Griffin, High Wycombe, 1977.

KING, W. H. *Statistics in Education.* Macmillan Education, Basingstoke, 1970.

LINDGREN, B. W. *Basic Ideas of Statistics.* Macmillan, New York, 1975. *Statistical Theory.* Macmillan, New York, 3rd edn, 1976.

LINDLEY, D. V. *Introduction to Probability and Statistics from a Bayesian Viewpoint.* Part 1, *Probability*; Part 2, *Inference.* Cambridge University Press, 1965. *Making Decisions.* Wiley, New York, 1971.

MAISEL, L. *Probability, Statistics and Random Processes.* Simon & Schuster, New York, 1971.

MAISTROV, L. E. *Probability Theory: a Historical Sketch.* Academic Press, 1974.

Mathematical Association. *An Approach to A-level Probability and Statistics.* Bell & Hyman, 1975.

MEDDIS, R. *Statistical Handbook for Non-statisticians.* McGraw-Hill, New York, 1975.

MOORE, D. S. *Statistics: Concepts and Controversies.* W. H. Freeman, Reading, 1979.

MOSTELLER, F. *Fifty Challenging Problems in Probability.* Addison-Wesley, 1965.

MOSTELLER, F., ROURKE, R. E. K. and THOMAS, G. B. *Probability with Statistical Applications.* Addison-Wesley, 1970.

MOSTELLER, F., et al. Statistics by Example Series. 1. *Detecting Patterns*; 2. *Exploring Data*; 3. *Finding Models*; 4. *Weighing Chances.* Addison-Wesley, 1973. A teacher's commentary is available for each volume.

Nuffield Mathematics Project, *Probability and Statistics.* W. & R. Chambers, Edinburgh/John Murray, 1969.

Open University, relevant texts from courses mentioned on pages 122–3.

PIAGET, J. and INHELDER, B. *The Origin of the Idea of Chance in Children.* Routledge & Kegan Paul, 1975.

POLLARD, J. H. *A Handbook of Numerical and Statistical Techniques.* Cambridge University Press, 1977.

QUENOUILLE, M. H. *Fundamentals of Statistical Reasoning.* Griffin, High Wycombe, 1965. *Rapid Statistical Calculations.* Griffin, High Wycombe, 1972.

RÅDE, L. *Statistics at the School Level.* Almqvist & Wiksell, Stockholm, and John Wiley, New York, 1975. *The Teaching of Probability and Statistics – the Proceedings of the Carbondale Conferences.* Almqvist & Wiksell, Stockholm, 1970. This includes some very interesting papers.

SERVAIS, W. and VARGA, T. *Teaching School Mathematics*. Penguin Books, Harmondsworth, 1971.

Schools Council History, Geography and Social Science 8–13 Project, *Games and Simulations in the Classroom*. Collins/ESL, Bristol, 1975.

Schools Council Mathematics for the Majority Project, *Luck and Judgement*. Hart-Davis Educational, St Albans, 1971.

SKIPWORTH, G. E. *Exercises and Worked Examples in Statistics*. Heinemann Educational Books, 1971.

SZMIDT, T. and BISSELL, A. F. *Statistical Teaching Aids*. Institute of Statisticians, 1977.

TANUR, J. (ed.). *Statistics – a Guide to the Unknown*. Holden-Day, San Francisco, 1972. A set of short essays on applications of statistics in many situations.

TAYLOR, J. and WALFORD, R. *Simulation in the Classroom*. Penguin Books, Harmondsworth, 1972.

TOCHER, K.D. *The Art of Simulation*. Hodder & Stoughton Educational, Dunton Green, 1969.

TODHUNTER, I. *A History of the Mathematical Theory of Probability from the Time of Pascal to that of Laplace*. Chelsea Publishing, New York, 1949.

WALKER, H. M. and LEV, J. *Elementary Statistical Methods*. Holt, Rinehart & Winston, New York, 3rd edn, 1969.

YATES, F. *Sampling Methods for Censuses and Surveys*. Griffin, High Wycombe, 1960.

YOUDEN, W. J. *Risk, Choice and Prediction*. Duxbury Press, Mass., 1974.

Statistics books for specific subjects

a Biology

BAILEY, N. T. J. *Statistical Methods in Biology*. Hodder & Stoughton Educational, Dunton Green, 1974.

BISHOP, O. N. *Statistics for Biology*. Longman, 1974.

CAMPBELL, R. *Statistics for Biologists*. Cambridge University Press, 1974.

Open University, S299 *Statistics for Genetics*. Open University Press, Milton Keynes, 1976–77.

PARKER, R. E. *Introductory Statistics for Biology*. Edward Arnold, 1973.

b Economics

ALLEN, R. G. D. *Statistics for Economists*. Hutchinson, 1972.

BLYTH, C. A. *The Use of Economic Statistics*. Allen & Unwin, 1960.

EDWARDS, B. *Sources of Economic and Business Statistics*. Heinemann Educational Books, 1972.

HEY, J. D. *Statistics in Economics*. Martin Robertson, Oxford, 1974.

JOLLIFFE, F. R. *Common Sense Statistics for Economists and Others*. Routledge & Kegan Paul, 1974.

LOWRY, J. H. *World Population and Food Supply*. Edward Arnold, 1975.

MAYES, A. C. and MAYES, D. G. *Introductory Economic Statistics*. John Wiley, New York, 1976.

Open University, MDT 241, units 10–13. *Descriptive and Economic Statistics*. Open University Press, Milton Keynes, 1974.

c Geography

DALTON, R., MINSHULL, R., GARLICK, J.and ROBINSON, A. *Correlation Techniques in Geography*. George Philip, 1976.

HAMMOND, R. and MCCULLAGH, P. S. *Quantitative Techniques in Geography*. Oxford University Press, 1978.

MOWFORTH, M. *Statistics for Geographers*. Harrap, 1980.

SMITH, D. M. *Patterns in the Human Geography*. Penguin Books, Harmondsworth, 1975.

WILSON, A. G. and KIRKBY, M. J. *Mathematics for Geographers and Planners*. Oxford University Press, 1975.

d History

FLOUD, R. *An Introduction to Quantitative Methods for Historians*. Methuen, 1973.

Open University, D301, units 1–4. *The Quantitative Analysis of Historical Data*. Open University Press, Milton Keynes, 1974.

e Social Sciences

ANDERSON, T. R. and ZELDITCH, M. *A Basic Course in Statistics with Sociological Implications*. Holt, Rinehart & Winston, New York, 1968.

CONNOLLY, T. G. and SLUCKIN, W. *An Introduction to Statistics for the Social Sciences*. Macmillan, 1971.

EDWARDS, B. *Sources of Social Statistics*. Heinemann Educational Books, 1974.

HAMMERTON, M. *Statistics for the Human Sciences*. Longman, 1975.

KALTON, G. *Introduction to Statistical Ideas for Social Scientists*. Chapman & Hall, 1966.

SIEGEL, S. *Non-parametric Statistics for the Behavioural Sciences*. McGraw-Hill New York, 1956.

YEOMANN, K. A. *Statistics for the Social Scientist*. 2 vols. 1. *Introducing Statistics*; 2. *Applied Statistics*. Penguin Books, Harmondsworth, 1968.

Statistical tables

BRAITHWAITE, G. R. and TITMUS, C. O. D. *Lanchester Short Statistical Tables*. Hodder & Stoughton, 1967.

DUNSTAN, F. D. J., NIX, A. B. J. and REYNOLDS, J. F. *Statistical Tables*. RND Publications, 1979.

Heinemann's Statistical Tables. Heinemann Educational Books, n.d.

FOWLIE, J. S. *Statistical Tables for Students*. Oliver & Boyd, Edinburgh, 1969.

KMIETOWICZ, Z. W. and YANNOULIS, Y. *Mathematical, Statistical and Financial Tables for the Social Sciences.* Longman, 1976.

LINDLEY, D. V. and MILLER, J. C. P. *Cambridge Elementary Statistical Tables.* Cambridge University Press, 1953.

MURDOCH, J. and BARNES, J. A. *Statistical Tables for Science, Engineering, Management and Business Studies.* Macmillan Education, Basingstoke, 2nd edn, 1971.

NEAVE, H. R. *Statistics Tables.* Allen & Unwin, 1978.

POWELL, F. C. *Cambridge Mathematical and Statistical Tables.* Cambridge University Press, 1976.

WHITE, J., YEATS, A, and SKIPWORTH, G. *Tables for Statisticians.* Stanley Thornes, 1974.

Guides to sources of secondary data (generally in most public libraries)

Central Statistical Office, *Government Statistics – a Brief Guide to Sources*, CSO, annually.

Facts in Focus. Penguin Books, Harmondsworth, 5th edn, 1980.

Committee of Librarians and Statisticians, *Recommended Basic UK Statistical Sources for Community Use.* Library Association, 3rd edn, 1975.

Recommended Basic Statistical Sources: International. Library Association, 1975.

Sources of secondary data

Everyone has a favourite source of reference material to answer questions that come up in conversation, whether it be *Pears Cyclopaedia, Whitaker's Almanack* or the *Guinness Book of Records.* The wealth of information now collected has become less easy to disseminate and impossible to condense into really manageable form. When researching to verify some point of inquiry, it is surprising how often the particular statistic you want is not in the publication where you might expect to find it. No panacea can be offered for this problem, but the following may be helpful: **1** a selection of compact bibliographies which are convenient to assemble, giving leads to the main official series (some comment on their recommendations is added, to help make good use of limited library funds); **2** a short list of periodicals and up-dating services to which it is possible to subscribe without inordinate expense; **3** a list of addresses of establishments that may be able to provide the necessary information.

1 Bibliographies

Even HM Stationery Office agents and librarians find the HMSO daily lists and catalogues unmanageable, but one official bibliography does help steer a path through the maze. A brief digest listing about a hundred series is obtainable annually from the Central Statistical Office under the title *Government Statistics: a Brief Guide to Sources.* This also includes prices and gives a useful list of government departments supplying information in the publications or to supplement them. A card folder *The United Kingdom in Figures* is also supplied annually. Both of these are free, and enough cards could be ordered for issue to students.

The Committee of Librarians and Statisticians, whose membership derives from the Library Association and Royal Statistical Society, has compiled *Recommended Basic UK Statistical Sources for Community Use* and *Recommended Basic Statistical Sources: International* with a different purpose in mind. The aim of this is to give guidance especially to county and borough librarians, as to which publications their collections should contain and, if that makes too heavy a call on resources, to suggest priorities within it. The list contains a little over half as many titles as *Government Statistics*, some of them from other sources (publisher and price are quoted). Besides the *Annual Abstract* and *Monthly Digest*, the weekly *Trade and Industry*, and relevant regional abstracts the basic list includes the United Nations *Statistical Yearbook* and material that now appears in *Social Trends* (annually). The list is worth having in spite of its tendency to date as publications are merged or renamed, and various series transferred between them.

For more detailed research, beyond the scope of most class projects unless these concentrate on a very narrow area, the Social Science Research Council together with the Royal Statistical Society is sponsoring a series of exhaustive annotated bibliographies (for example there will eventually be eight or more on transport alone) which come as close to the last word on guides to sources as any series is ever likely to do. These are published by Heinemann under the collective title *Reviews of UK Statistical Sources*.

More limited and selective in scope is the Open University D291 course material on statistical sources, but some of the points drawn out in these texts could be used with younger students if the more sophisticated applications were left aside. The libraries in the Departments of Trade and Industry and the Environment issue their own bibliographies which are invaluable to anyone wishing to do more detailed research in these fields.

2 Periodicals

In considering how far to follow the Library Association's advice, smaller school libraries may find subscriptions to the *Monthly Digest* and *Annual Abstract* expensive. The former is valuable in giving some seasonal data and in being generally the more up to date, though covering a shorter time span; a possible solution is to take one or two issues per year. The *Annual Abstract* includes some of the same series and some additional ones, which eventually permit retrieval of continuous time series on any one topic. A cheaper, much less detailed alternative is the CSO *Facts in Focus* (Penguin Books, 5th edn, 1980). The Library Association list recommendation of the *Abstract of Regional Statistics* (or in Wales, *Digest of Welsh Statistics*) is worth taking seriously because comparison of regional with national figures is often illuminating in teaching just how much these aggregates can show of the effects of local habits and patterns. The other recommendation, *Social Trends*, covers a very wide range of interesting subject matter and is well presented. Though it costs a little more than the more conventionally presented *Annual Abstract*, it highlights many detailed interrelationships (within a less exhaustive field) and its emphasis on social implications is probably of more value for school use.

A surprising omission from the Library Association's basic list is the annual *National Income and Expenditure* blue book. It is of course in their extended list, but could be regarded as essential for any school teaching economics. On population data, the *Preliminary Report* of each decennial census is well worth having, with numbers of people by counties and districts compared with those ten years before, and special tables showing conurbation and new town trends. County reports contain different figures which could contribute to any local demographic project work. There are now sixteen more compact annual series replacing the former bulky three-volume Registrar General's *Statistical Review*, including one on population estimates and projections; the others are rather specialized for the general user. The former *Quarterly Return* has also been replaced by the quarterly publication *Population Trends*, a convenient summary of the whole field of vital statistics. There is also the *Monitors* series on individual topics (details from the Office of Population Censuses and Surveys (address below)).

Transport specialists may wish to consider *Transport Statistics*. Detailed work on the retail price index can usefully be supported by referring to the *Family Expenditure Survey Report* (published annually). The CSO *Statistical News* (quarterly) provides a general up-dating service on news of official data and some more detailed explanatory articles. The Treasury *Economic Progress Report* (monthly), distributed by the Central Office of Information, gives tabulated and graphed data of several important economic series (free mailing list). The Department of Energy's monthly *Energy Trends* would be invaluable for anyone using energy data in project work. The Department of Employment's *Employment News* (monthly) is less detailed but includes some useful material.

In addition to the official sources of data supplied on an England and Wales or UK basis, many local authorities, especially metropolitan counties, publish data for their area in a convenient and useful form. It is not feasible to catalogue this here, but the publications of the Greater London Council are of wider interest as, besides being exceptionally extensive in range and content, they directly affect a larger population than any other authority. The GLC publishes its own *Annual Abstract*, a volume comparable in scope to that for Great Britain. For everyday purposes in school the diagrammatic summary *London Facts and Figures* (5th edn, 1978) is strongly recommended.

Another valuable source of economic data is from the bank reviews. These are available free from each of the 'big four' banks, and often contain good examples of diagrammatic presentation as well as data. The Bank of England also produces its *Quarterly Bulletin*, which is more detailed than the usual bank review.

3 Useful addresses
Bank of England, Economic Intelligence Department, Threadneedle Street, London EC2 8AH

Barclays Bank Group Economic Intelligence Unit, 54 Lombard Street, London EC3P 3AH

British Gas Corporation, Rivermill House, 152 Grosvenor Road, London SW1V 3JL

British Railways Board, Chief Publicity Officer, 222 Marylebone Road, London NW1

Central Electricity Generating Board, Information Services, 15 Newgate Street, London EC1

Central Office of Information, Circulation Manager (Publications), Hercules Road, London SE1

Central Statistical Office (CSO) Great George Street, London SW1P 3AQ

Department of Employment (News and Information) 12 St James's Square, London SW1Y 4LL

Department of Energy (Information Division) Thames House South, Millbank, London SW1P 4QJ

Department of the Environment, 2 Marsham Street, London SW1P 3EB

Department of Health and Social Security, 14 Russell Square, London WC1B 5EP

Department of Trade and Industry, Statistics and Market Intelligence Library, Export House, 50 Ludgate Hill, London EC4M 7HU

Electricity Council, 30 Millbank, London SW1P 4RD

English Tourist Board, 4 Grosvenor Gardens, London SW1W ODU

H M Stationery Office, P O Box 569, London SE1 9NH

Institute of Statisticians, 36 Churchgate Street, Bury St Edmunds, Suffolk, 1P3 31RD

Library Association, 7 Ridgmount Street, London WC1E 7AE

Lloyds Bank Ltd, 71 Lombard Street, London EC3P 3BS

Midland Bank Ltd, Economics Department, Poultry, London, EC2P 2BX

Ministry of Agriculture, Fisheries and Food, Whitehall Place, London SW1A 2HH

National Coal Board, Public Relations Department, Hobart House, Grosvenor Place, London SW1

National Savings Committee, Education Branch, Alexandra House, Kingsway, London WC2B 6TS

National Water Council, 1 Queen Anne's Gate, London SW1H 9BT

National Westminster Bank Ltd, Market Intelligence Department, 41 Lothbury, London EC2P 2BP

Office of Population Censuses and Surveys, (Information Branch), St Catherine's House, 10 Kingsway, London WC2B 6JP

Open University, Director of Marketing, P O Box 81, Milton Keynes MK7 6AT

Post Office, Publicity Division, Union House, St Martins-le-Grand, London EC1A 1AR (Marketing Department, R551)

Royal Statistical Society, 25/26 Enford Street, London W1

ARTICLES

Teaching at the school level

BEAUMONT, G. 'The teaching of statistics – Stage C', *Mathematics Teaching*, 21, 1962, 15–18. (See also C. HOPE for the first two articles in this series.)

BROWN, M. 'Visual aids for teaching statistics', *Mathematics in School*, 3, 2, 1974, 31–2.

BUNT, L. N. H. 'Probability and statistical inference in the secondary school', *Dialectica*, 21, 1967, 366–82. (An account of the author's own syllabus used in Holland.)

CONWAY, F. 'Statistics in schools', *Trends in Education*, 4, 1975, 34–7.

DAVIES, H. M. 'Practical experimentation in the teaching of statistics at the secondary school level', *Sigma*, April 1967, 5–10.

DOWNTON, F. 'Statistics at A level – a reappraisal', *Royal Statistical Society Journal*, Series A, 131, 1968, 500–29.

EVANS, I. G. 'Statistics in A level mathematics syllabuses', Research memoir no. 8, Department of Statistics, University College of Wales, Aberystwyth, 1973.

FISCHBEIN, E., *et. al.* 'Effects of age and instruction on combinatory ability in children', *British Journal of Educational Psychology*, 40, 1970, 261–70.

FISHBEIN, E., PAMPU, I. and MINZÀT, I. 'Initiation aux probabilités a l'école élémentaire', *Educational Studies in Mathematics*, 2, 1969, 16–31.

FISHBEIN, E., BARBAT, I. and MINZÀT, I. 'Intuitions primaires et intuitions secondaires dans l'initiation aux probabilités', *Educational Studies in Mathematics*, 4, 1971, 264–80.

FISCHER, F. E. 'Empirical evidence for the central limit theorem: a classroom demonstration', *Mathematics Teacher*, LXIV, 1971, 415–17.

GRASS, B. A. 'Statistics made simple', *Arithmetic Teacher*, 12, 1965, 196–8.

HARRIS, B. 'Lucky Jim', Mathematics Teaching, 66, 1974, 39–42.

HARRISON, R. D. 'An activity approach to the teaching of statistics and probability' (in three parts), *Mathematics Teaching*, 1966, 34, 31–8; 35, 52–61; 36, 57–65.

HOLMES, P. 'Using computers in the teaching of statistics', *Mathematical Gazette*, 59, 410, 1975, 228–46.

HOLMES, P. '... but is it statistics?', *Mathematics in School*, 5, 2, 1976, 15–16.

HOPE, C. 'The teaching of statistics – Stage A'. *Mathematics Teaching*, 15, 1961, 29–34.

HOPE, C. 'The teaching of statistics – Stage B', *Mathematics Teaching*, 18, 1962, 17–21. (See also G. BEAUMONT. These articles give suggested examples rather than a coherent philosophy.)

KERSLAKE, D. 'Some children's views on probability', *Mathematics in School*, 3, 4, 1974, 22.

KIEFER, J. 'Statistical inference', *Mathematical Spectrum*, 3, 1, 1970, 1–11.

MORLEY, A. 'A new development in primary school mathematics', *Mathematics Teaching*, 70, 1975, 15–17. (A look at the Dutch IOWO work [Institut

Ontwikkeling Wiskunde Onderwijs (Institute for the Development of Mathematical Education)]. See IOWO, *Look on Luck*, IOWO, Utrecht, 1974.)

OGBORN, J. 'How the normal distribution got its hump', *Mathematics Teaching*, 66, 1974. 53–5.

O'TOOLE, A. L. 'Probability and statistics teaching in Western European secondary schools', *American Statistician*, 20, 2, 1966, 23–4.

RAO, C. R. 'A multidisciplinary approach for teaching statistics and probability', *International Journal of Mathematical Education in Science and Technology*, 2, 1971, 295–312. (This is also in Råde's book of the Carbondale Conference (1970).)

RAO, C. R. 'Teaching of statistics at the secondary level: an interdisciplinary approach', *International Journal of Mathematical Education in Science and Technology*, 6, 2, 1975, 151–62.

SELKIRK, J. 'Statistics as a sixth form subject', *Newcastle Institute of Education Journal*, November 1972, 45–6.

SIMON, J. L. and HOLMES, A. 'A new way to teach probability and statistics', *Mathematics Teacher*, LXII, 1969, 283–8. (By using Monte Carlo methods.)

SPEED, T. P. 'Statistics in school and society', *Mathematical Spectrum*, 6, 1, 1973, 7–11.

SPITZNAGEL, E. L. 'An experimental approach in the teaching of probability', *Mathematics Teacher*, LXI, 1968, 565–8.

TAGG, D. 'The teaching of probability and statistics in the sixth form', *Bulletin of the Institute of Mathematics and its Applications*, 7, 8, 1971, 253.

VARGA, T. 'Logic and probability in the lower grades', *Educational Studies in Mathematics*, 4, 1972, 346–57.

WILKINSON, J. D. and NELSON, D. 'Probability and statistics, trial teaching in sixth grade', *Arithmetic Teacher*, 13, 1966, 100–106.

WILKS, S. S. 'Teaching statistical inference in elementary mathematics curricular', *American Mathematical Monthly*, 6, 5, 1958, 143–53.

Examples and applications

BARR, D. R. 'When will the next record rainfall occur?', *Mathematics Magazine*, 45, 1972, 15–19.

CALLENDER, L. 'Speed trapping', *Mathematics Teaching*, 45, 1968, 41.

CAMPBELL, C. and JOINER, B. L. 'How to get the answer without being sure you've asked the question', *American Statistician*, 27, 5, 1973, 229–31. (How many of your students smoke pot? A simple design to find out without incriminating.)

CLARKE, R. H. 'Let's form a queue', *Mathematics Teaching*, 56, 1971, 28–33.

CLIFF, A. D. and ORD, J. K. 'Model building and the analysis of spatial pattern in human geography', *Royal Statistical Society Journal*, Series A, 137, 1975, 297–349.

DESSART, D. J. 'To tip a waiter – a problem in unordered selections with repetitions', *Mathematics Teacher*, LXIV, 1971, 307–310.

ENGEL, A. 'Teaching probability in intermediate grades', *International Journal of Mathematical Education in Science and Technology*, **2**, 1971, 243–94. (Some interesting simulations. This article is also in Råde's book of the Carbondale Conference (1970).)

EWENS, W. J. 'A biologist's magic urn', *Mathematical Spectrum*, **11**, 2, 1978, 41–4.

FLETCHER, A. A. 'Correlation of seeding and placing at Wimbledon – a classroom exercise', *Mathematics Teaching*, 73, 1975, 44–6.

FLETCHER, C. R. 'Probability of acute angled triangles', *Mathematical Gazette*, **LV**, 394, 1971, 421–2.

FOX, R. M. 'Statistics projects outside the classroom', *Mathematical Gazette*, **LVII**, 401, 1973, 165–9.

FRANKLIN, M. 'Teaching statistics in schools: survey on pocket money', *The Statistician*, **17**, 1, 1967, 73–80.

GAGER, T. A. 'Statistics and plant ecology', *School Science Review*, **55**, 192, 1974, 500–503.

GODSAVE, G. F. 'David's navel', *Mathematics Teaching*, 61, 1972, 28–9. (Studies on the Golden ratio in human beings.)

GOLDSTEIN, G. 'A classroom approach to simulation', *Mathematics Teaching*, 49, 1969, 14–21.

GOOD, I. G. 'Statistics and today's problems', *American Statistician*, **26**, 3, 1972, 11–19.

GREENFIELD, T. 'Blindfold climbers', *Teaching Statistics*, **1**, 1, 1979, 15–19.

HART, R. A., HUTTON, J and SHAROT, T. 'A statistical analysis of association football matches', *Applied Statistics*, **24**, 1, 1975, 17–27.

HARVEY, P. 'Stylistic analysis – the mathematical determination of authorship', *Mathematical Gazette*, **LIV**, 390, 1970, 361–8.

HILL, L. and ROTHERY, A. 'Two probability simulations', *Mathematics Teaching*, 73, 1975, 27–9.

HILLE, J. W. 'A Bayesian look at the jury service', *Mathematical Spectrum*, **11**, 2, 1978, 45–7.

HOLMES, A. H. 'Statistical inference: some classroom activities', *School Science and Mathematics*, **LXXI**, 1971, 75–8.

KAPADIA, R. 'The politics of inflation', *Bulletin in Applied Statistics*, **3**, 1, 1976, 64–74.

KAYE, D. 'Investigation in and around the game of craps', *Mathematics Teaching*, 41, 1967, 9–16.

KAYE, D. 'Lies, damned lies and one-tailed tests', *Mathematics Teaching*, 59, 1972, 13–15.

KING, C. A. M. 'Mathematics in geography', *International Journal of Mathematical Education in Science and Technology*, **1**, 1970, 185–205.

LANGNER, A. J. 'Statistical evaluation of π', *Mathematical Gazette*, **L**, 371, 1966, 19–21.

LAWRENCE, A. E. 'Playing with probability', *Mathematical Gazette*, **LIII**, 386, 1969, 347–54.

LAWRENCE, A. E. 'Playing with probability. Return match', *Mathematical Gazette*, **LV**, 391, 1971, 49–50.

LEIBOWITZ, M. A. 'Queues', *Scientific American*, August 1968, 96–103.

MALPAS, A. J. 'Mathematical interpretation of experimental data in schools', *International Journal of Mathematical Education in Science and Technology*, **4**, 1973, 329–33.

MILLER, P. J. 'Markov chains and chemical processes', *Education in Chemistry*, **9**, 1972, 222–4.

MORRIS, M. 'Teaching statistics in schools: a family topic' *The Statistician*, **18**, 1, 1968, 25–30.

O'BRIAN, T. C. and BUDDE, P. 'Hypothesis testing: a classroom activity', *Mathematics Teaching*, 69, 1974, 38–9.

PAGE, P. J. 'Do bristlebacks cluster?', *Teaching Statistics*, **1**, 1, 1979, 8–11.

PINHEY, J. G. L. 'The Comte de Buffon's paper clip', *Mathematics Gazette*, **LIV**, 1970, 288.

RÅDE, L. 'Probability and flow graphs', *International Journal of Mathematical Education in Science and Technology*, **4**, 1973, 455–92.

SELKIRK, K. 'Random models in the classroom', *Mathematics in School*, **2**, 6, 1973, 5–6; **3**, 1, 1974, 5–7; **3**, 2, 1974, 15–17.

SIMONS, J. A. E. 'A new triangle on the election', *Mathematical Gazette*, **LI**, 378, 1967, 291–4.

SMITHERS, G. S. 'Public opinion polls in schools', *Mathematical Gazette*, **LV**, 391, 1971, 28–34.

SMITHERS, G. S. 'Early warning', *Mathematical Gazette*, **LVI**, 397, 1972, 188–94.

SPARROW, A. E. 'Teaching statistics in schools: drinking survey', *The Statistician*, **18**, 2, 1968, 157–61.

TAMMADGE, A. 'How much does it cost to keep a dog?', *Mathematics Teaching*, 57, 1971, 9–11.

VARGA, T. 'Boxes, marbles and tables', *Mathematics Teaching*, 50, 1970, 36–7.

WATSON, D. 'On scoring in games', *Mathematical Gazette*, **LIV**, 388, 1970, 110–13.

WATSON, F. R. 'Three games', *Mathematics in School*, **2**, 3, 1973, 27–9.

WELLS, P. 'Decaying pennies', *Mathematics Teaching*, 53, 1970, 2–3.

WILKINSON, R. K. 'Statistics in sixth form economics', *Teaching Statistics*, **1**, 1, 1979, 14–23.

WILLIAMS, C. B. 'Mendenhall's studies of word length distribution in works of Shakespeare and Bacon', *Biometrike*, **62**, 1, 1975, 207–12.

WYVILL, R. 'Friday the thirteenth', *Mathematics in School*, **2**, 4, 1973, 29.

WYVILL, R. '1900 and all that', *Mathematics in School*, **3**, 6, 1974, 31.

Theory relevant at school level

ANDERSON, D. V. 'The deviation test', *Mathematical Gazette*, **LII**, 386, 1969, 380–7.

BACKHOUSE, J. K. 'A simple introduction to tests of significance', *Mathematical Gazette*, **LV**, 391, 1971, 1–4.

BAILEY, B. J. R. 'Estimation from first principles', *Mathematical Gazette*, **LVII**, 401, 1973, 169–74.

BEAUMONT, G. P. 'What's the odds?', *Mathematics Teaching*, 66, 1974, 46–7.

BUXTON, R. 'Probability and its measurement', *Mathematics Teaching*, 49, 1969, 4–13; 50, 1970, 56–63.

CLARKE, L. E. 'Down with the mean', *Mathematical Gazette*, **LV**, 393, 1971, 286–98.

CONWAY, F. 'A graphical approach to regression analysis', *Mathematics Teaching*, 53, 1970, 7–11.

DUDLEY, B. A. C. 'The mathematical basis of population genetics', *International Journal of Mathematical Education in Science and Technology*, **4**, 1973, 363–72.

ELLIS, L. E. 'A note on the application of the chi-squared test', *Mathematical Gazette*, **LIV**, 1970, 397–9.

ENGEL, A. 'Teaching probability in intermediate grades', *International Journal of Mathematical Education in Science and Technology*, **2**, 1971, 243–94.

ENGEL, A. 'Outline of a problem oriented, computer oriented and applications oriented High School mathematics course', *International Journal of Mathematical Education in Science and Technology*, **4**, 1973, 455–92.

FORSYTH, F. G. 'The practical construction of a chain price index number', *Royal Statistical Society Journal*, Series A, **141**, Part 3, 1978, 348–58.

FREUDENTHAL, H. 'The empirical law of large numbers. The stability of frequencies', *Educational Studies in Mathematics*, **4**, 1972, 484–90.

FREUDENTHAL, H. 'The crux of course design in probability', *Educational Studies in Mathematics*, **5**, 1974, 261–77.

GANI, J. 'Gambling and probability', *Mathematical Spectrum*, **4**, 1, 1972, 9–14.

GRIFFITHS, I. D. 'Simulating the value of π', *Bulletin in Applied Statistics*, **2**, 2, 1975, 39–45.

KAUFMAN, B. and RÅDE, L. 'Relations and probability', *Educational Studies in Mathematics*, **5**, 1973, 49–64.

MOORE, P. G. 'Sampling and opinion polls', *Mathematical Spectrum*, **3**, 2, 1971, 61–6.

NELSON, R. D. 'Undistributed middle – a question of probability', *Mathematics Teaching*, 46, 1969, 34–5.

OAKLEY, B. E. and PERRY, R. L. 'A sampling process', *Mathematical Gazette*, **XLIX**, 367, 1965, 42–4.

PARADINE, C. G. 'The probability distribution of χ^2', *Mathematical Gazette*, **L**, 371, 1966, 8–18.

PLACKETT, R. L. 'The application of the chi-squared test', *Mathematical Gazette*, **LV**, 394, 1971, 363–6.

PRESCOTT, P. 'Further comments on error techniques', *Mathematics Teaching*, 57, 1971, 6–8.

QUADLING, D. and CABLE, J. 'Correlation coefficients in the same segment by vectors', *Mathematical Gazette*, **LVIII**, 402, 1973, 307–11.

RÅDE, L. 'A probabilistic triangle problem', *Mathematical Spectrum*, **2**, 2, 1970, 57–64.

RAO, T. J. 'Sample survey techniques and their applications', *Mathematical Spectrum*, **3**, 2, 1971, 57–61.

SELKIRK, K. E. 'An approach to the normal curve', *Mathematics Teaching*, 62, 1979, 44–5.

SHERLOCK, A. J. 'Experimental theory at school', *Mathematical Gazette*, **XLIX**, 367, 1965, 39–40.

SHERLOCK, A. 'New techniques in logic and probability', *Mathematics Teaching*, 67, 1974, 52–6.

TRURAN, T. D. 'An analysis of the game of odds', *Mathematics Teaching*, 15, 1968, 38–40.

WILD, J. V. 'Samples', *Mathematics Teaching*, 47, 1969, 15.

Reports

American Statistical Association. 'Report on the Committee for Probability and Statistics in the Secondary School', *American Statistician*, **18**, 4, 1964, 17–25.

LINDLEY, D. V. 'A report on university staff and students in statistics', *Royal Statistical Society Journal*, Series A, **129**, 1966, 467–70.

MOSTELLER, F. 'Progress report of the Joint Committee of the Statistical Association and the National Council of Teachers of Mathematics', *Mathematics Teacher*, March 1970, 199–208.

ROSENBAUM, S. 'A report on the use of statistics in social science research', *Royal Statistical Society Journal*, Series A, **134**, 1971, 534–610.

Royal Statistical Society. 'The teaching of statistics in schools', *Royal Statistical Society Journal*, Series A, **115**, 1952, 126–37.

Royal Statistical Society. 'The teaching of statistics: a symposium', *Royal Statistical Society Journal*, Series A, **127**, 1964, 199–233.

Royal Statistical Society. 'Interim report of the RSS Committee on the Teaching of Statistics in Schools', *Royal Statistical Society Journal*, Series A, **131**, 1968, 478–99.

Royal Statistical Society. 'Report of joint committee on "Teaching of Statistics", and discussion', *Royal Statistical Society Journal*, Series A, **137**, 1974, 412–27.

General

BENJAMIN, B. 'Teaching statistics and operational research to civil servants', *American Statistician*, **26**, 4, 1972, 23–6.

BISSEL, A. F. and HOBSON, T. F. J. 'Learning and teaching statistics by correspondence', *The Statistician*, **18**, 1968, 237–44.

COHEN, J. 'Subjective probability', *Scientific American*, **197**, 1957, 128–34.

DOWNTON, F. and LOCKWOOD, C. 'Computer studies of baccarat I: Chemin-de-fer', *Royal Statistical Society Journal*, Series A, **138**, 1965, 228–38.

EHRENBERG, A. S. C. 'Mathematics and statistics', *Bulletin in Applied Statistics*, **2**, 2, 1975, 1–6.

EHRENBERG, A. S. C. 'Rudiments of numeracy', *Royal Statistical Society Journal*, Series A, **140**, 1977, 277–97.

FAINBERG, W. E. 'Teaching the Type I and Type II errors: the judicial process', *American Statistician*, **25**, 3, 1971, 30–2.

FOLKS, J. L. 'Some prior probabilities on the future of statistics', *American Statistician*, **24**, 5, 1970, 10–12.

GANI, J. 'Whodunit? or the Reverend Mr Bayes FRS helps to decide', *Mathematical Spectrum*, 1, 1966, 9–13.

GANI, J. 'Statistics in everyday life', *Mathematics in School*, **2**, 5, 1973, 2–5.

GARDNER, M. 'The rambling random walk and its gambling equivalent', *Scientific American*, May 1969, 118–20.

GRASS, B. A. 'Statistics made simple', *Arithmetic Teacher*, **12**, 1965, 196–8.

HARRIS, P. T. 'Some statistical aspects of opinion polling and election forecasting', *Bulletin in Applied Statistics*, **2**, 1, 1975, 44–51.

HEALY, M. J. R. 'Is statistics a science?', *Royal Statistical Society Journal*, Series A, **141**, Part 3, 1978, 385–93.

HOGG, R. V. 'On statistical education', *American Statistician*, **26**, 3, 1972, 8–11.

KENDALL, M. G. and MURCHLAND, J. D. 'Statistical aspects of the legality of gambling', *Royal Statistical Society Journal*, Series A, **127**, 1964, 359–83.

KENDALL, M. G. 'The future of statistics – a second look', *Royal Statistical Society Journal*, Series A, **131**, 1968, 182–204.

KENDALL, M. G. 'The early history of index numbers', *International Statistical Review*, **37**, 1969. 1–12.

KRUSKEL, W. 'The ubiquity of statistics', *American Statistician*, **28**, 1, 1974, 3–6.

LANGNER, W. L. 'Checks on population growth 1750–1850', *Scientific American*, **226**, 2, 1972, 93–9.

LINDLEY, D. V. 'Professor Hogben's "crisis" – a survey of the foundations of statistics', *Applied Statistics*, **7**, 1958, 186–98.

MOSTELLER, F. 'What has happened to probability in the high school?', *Mathematics Teacher*, 55, 1961, 824–31.

ORE, O. 'Pascal and the invention of probability', *American Mathematical Monthly*, **67**, 1960, 409–19.

RÅDE, L. 'A bibliography on the teaching of probability and statistics', *Zentralblatt fur Didaktik der Mathematick*, 2, 1972, 70–2.

SALSBURG, D. S. 'Sufficiency and waste of information', *American Statistician*, **27**, 4, 1973, 152–4.

SWIRES-HENNESSY, E. 'Some problems of collecting statistics at the B.S.O.', *Bulletin in Applied Statistics*, **3**, 1, 1976, 30–8.

WARD, D. H. 'Weights and measures and the EEC', *Royal Statistical Society Journal*, Series A, **138**, 1975, 170–204.

WELCH, B. L. 'Statistics – a vocational or a cultural study', *Royal Statistical Society Journal*, Series A, **133**, 1970, 531–54.

Project team and consultative committee

Project team

Director
Peter Holmes

Deputy Director
G. Neil Rubra (1975–78)
Daphne Turner (1978–81)

Project Officers
Ramesh Kapadia (1975–79)
Alan Graham (1976–77)
Barbara Cox (1979–80)

Consultative committee

Professor J. P. C. Roach (Chairman)	Institute of Education, University of Sheffield
Professor V. Barnett	Department of Probability and Statistics, University of Sheffield
Dr C. Burstall	Deputy Director, National Foundation for Educational Research
M. Calvert (to March 1978)	Deputy Head, Ryshworth Middle School, Bingley, West Yorkshire
D. L. Davies (from March 1978)	Headmaster, Christopher Whitehead Boys' Secondary School, Worcester
R. Dimes	Vice-Principal, South Devon Technical College
Professor F. Downton	Department of Mathematics and Statistics, University of Birmingham
J. H. Durran	Head of Mathematics, Winchester College
G. S. Foster (from March 1978)	Head, The Towers School, Ashford, Kent
A. Hanley (from January 1979)	General Education Inspector for Mathematics, Northamptonshire
J. I. Hoyland (from January 1978)	formerly Head of Department for Non-examination Courses, King Ecgbert Comprehensive School, Sheffield
Miss J. Keen	Statistician, GEC Hirst Research Centre, Wembley
W. Maltby	Head of Mathematics, Toot Hill Comprehensive School, Bingham, Nottinghamshire

143

Mrs E. J. Mann — Mathematics Department, North Oxfordshire Technical College and School of Art

A. Owen — H M Inspectorate of Schools

P. Reynolds (to September 1978) — Mathematics Adviser, Suffolk

S. E. Rhodes (to December 1977) — Head, Colne High School, Brightlingsea, Essex

F. G. Richards (to July 1980) — Warden, Hackney Teachers' Centre

† Dr J. Selkirk — formerly Senior Sixth-form Tutor, High School, Gosforth

A. R. Stephenson — Secretary, University of London School Examinations Department

Schools Council

Mrs J. A. Denyer (from September 1976) — Curriculum Officer

W. M. Caldow (to August 1976) — Curriculum Officer

David Clemson (from April 1979) — Educational Researcher

Sue MacIntyre — Senior Project Editor

Graham Tall (to March 1979) — Educational Researcher

Murray Ward (to March 1977) — Educational Researcher